GROWING
WITH
GRATITUDE

GROWING WITH GRATITUDE

BUILDING RESILIENCE, HAPPINESS AND MENTAL WELLBEING
IN OUR SCHOOLS AND HOMES

ASH MANUEL

WILEY

First published in 2023 by John Wiley & Sons Australia, Ltd

Level 1, 155 Cremorne St, Richmond Vic 3121

Typeset in Palatino LT Std 11pt/15pt

© John Wiley & Sons Australia, Ltd 2023

The moral rights of the author have been asserted

ISBN: 978-1-119-89184-0

Cover design by Wiley
Cover Images: © Nikolaeva/Shutterstock,
© Foxys Graphic/Shutterstock

Disclaimer
The material in this publication is of the nature of general comment only, and does not represent professional advice. It is not intended to provide specific guidance for particular circumstances and it should not be relied on as the basis for any decision to take action or not take action on any matter which it covers. Readers should obtain professional advice where appropriate, before making any such decision. To the maximum extent permitted by law, the author and publisher disclaim all responsibility and liability to any person, arising directly or indirectly from any person taking or not taking action based on the information in this publication.

SKY94B48183-9474-4019-B003-D4F4C4EB9110_091222

This book is dedicated to Jason 'Lehmo' Lehmann,
Brooke Jeffs and Nigel Osborn.

CONTENTS

CONTENTS

ABOUT THE AUTHOR

Ash Manuel is passionate about positive education.

He is the founder of Growing with Gratitude, a wellbeing program and platform that teaches people in schools, organisations, workplaces, sports teams and at home the happiness and resilience skills they need to build and protect their mental wellbeing long into the future.

Ash's experience in education and sports coaching spans 25 years. It was in 2010, while working as a primary school physical education teacher in Adelaide, South Australia, that he discovered a number of people who excelled in their chosen field had identified gratitude and happiness as the keys to their success and achievement.

Through further investigation he discovered an entire new world: that of positive psychology. His greatest learning was that resilience and happiness are things you can actually practise. After a number of personal breakthroughs using these skills in his own life, he questioned, *Why don't we learn these skills back in primary school, when we are young?*

So that's exactly what he set out to do.

Today, Ash is widely regarded as a leader in positive education. His programs and resources have reached close to half a million students across the globe, as well as elite sports teams, and are currently accessed in 45 countries.

He has interviewed and hosted many high-profile people on The Positive Education Podcast, is often seen in the media and presents at numerous wellbeing conferences.

Ash believes gratitude, kindness, empathy, positive reflection, self-awareness, ownership and serving others are key building blocks to resilience and happiness. These are skills he practises on a daily basis, whether it's through personal reflection, by facilitating a gratitude game in the classroom or while playing social T12 cricket with mates.

growingwithgratitude.com

FOREWORD

How grateful am I for the positive contribution that this book affords in prioritising wellbeing as a shared educational community responsibility.

From my initial collaboration with the author Ash Manuel on a whole school *Growing with Gratitude: Exploring a school community's gratitude approach and influence on student wellbeing and achievement* research project (Price, Green & Manuel, University of South Australia, 2014/15), I have been personally and professionally enriched by his passion, positive outlook, happiness, determination and deep belief in wellbeing.

In this book, Ash advocates wellbeing as the foundation to one's sense of self and identity, feelings of belonging and connectedness to others, spaces and places, and personal and collective achievements. This book prioritises preventative and hopeful messages as Ash models the importance of self-care by his self-awareness of personal lived experiences and integrating educational and positive psychological strategies for personal development and growth that are best facilitated and sustained through not only individual agency, but also through shared whole school, home and broader community endeavours.

Nurturing Wellbeing Development in Education (McCallum & Price Eds., 2016) has been growing as a priority amidst the predominant emphasis on quality learning and academic achievement on global, national and local measures, with increasing evidence that *Well Teachers* supports *Well Students* (McCallum & Price, 2010), and the critical importance of teacher wellbeing (McCallum, Price, Graham & Morrison, 2020) and examining the *Ecological influences on teachers' wellbeing and 'fitness'* (Price & McCallum, 2015). However, given COVID-19 influences, wellbeing has risen in status, emerging as an essential pillar in educational philosophy, with evidence of the immense power of altruistic and pro-social acts such as habits of happiness and expressions of gratitude through community acts of helping one another.

What I love about this book is how Ash invites everyone, including students, parents/carers, educators, educational community members and himself, to take time to self-reflect on one's own wellbeing. That is, to appreciate the richness and learnings from life experiences, having a growth mindset and resilience in turning challenging experiences into positive opportunities, and taking time to recognise and acknowledge the strengths and contributions of those around them.

The positive wellbeing and educational outcomes of whole school, community, family and individual engagement with the strategies outlined in this book over recent years, is testament to Ash's advocacy and impact in scaffolding self-empowerment in responsibility of our own sustained wellbeing. Further, Ash promotes the significant benefits for self and others through supporting the wellbeing of significant others and expressing gratefulness for acts of kindness.

As you immerse yourself in these engaging chapters, Ash and I challenge you in continuing to build advocacy in championing the importance of wellbeing as fundamental to optimal learning, societal engagement and sustained wellbeing. An individual approach to wellbeing is important, however a collective commitment to self and others' wellbeing can ultimately foster a thriving and prosperous community.

We are grateful for your commitment to wellbeing of self and others and Ash provides practical suggestions throughout *Growing with Gratitude*.

Dr Deborah Price

Senior Lecturer Inclusive Education and Wellbeing
Research Degrees Coordinator
Centre for Research in Educational and
Social Inclusion (CRESI) Education Futures,
University of South Australia

President,
Australian Curriculum
Studies Association (ACSA)

INTRODUCTION

Hi Ash

We have had major issues at school lately with students having thoughts of suicide; we have increasing levels of self-harm and we have students trying to help each other and access support.

It is really becoming a massive concern. I have never, in my whole time at a school, had to support so many young people who are just dealing with such horrendous things, nor have I called ambulance and police so many times in one week before.

This is an extract from an actual email I received in June 2021 from a wellbeing coordinator at a high school (for the purpose of confidentiality, I won't name the school).

It's quite frightening, right?

Yet, I know for a fact that this is not a standalone case.

There are many other teachers, principals, educators—and parents—who have either experienced an escalating situation like this or are worried about experiencing one. Many of us report that we feel so utterly helpless when it comes to the mental health and wellbeing of our youngest, and most vulnerable, generation.

And who could blame us?

Over the past few years, we have been in and out of lockdowns; we've had interstate and overseas borders open and then close; jobs have been lost; vaccinations have been rolled out at record rates; sports have been suspended; and other social and community events have been impacted. All of this uncertainty and unrest has understandably affected our wellbeing like never before—and especially the mental health of our kids.

According to the United Nations Educational Scientific and Cultural Organisation (UNESCO), 1.38 billion—yes, *billion*—learners were impacted by school closures worldwide during the pandemic.

Meanwhile, latest statistics report that one in five parents or carers said they needed mental health and wellbeing support for their children. Of those, 73.2 per cent said they actually sought help. Yet, of those seeking help, 40.9 per cent said it was either difficult or very difficult to access mental health support.

Can you hear the alarm bells ringing?

There's no doubt that as an educator, a student, a parent, even a human being, times are challenging—and will continue to be. But there is hope.

As someone at the forefront of looking after our next generation, you have an amazing opportunity to create an environment that teaches and encourages students to practise adaptable thinking and emotional regulation to enhance children's resilience skills. You and the teams at your school can achieve this by setting up a strong, robust whole-school approach to positive education and wellbeing, and an environment where students and staff all feel they belong and can thrive.

Now, I won't lie. In the past this would have sounded like a lot of positive mumbo jumbo. But we've come a long way over the years.

In Australia, the BreakThrough Mental Health Research Foundation reported that 50 per cent of diagnosable mental illness onsets occur in children between the ages of 11 and 14; and 75 per cent of diagnosable mental illness onsets before age 24. So we know early intervention is crucial, and we're starting to make headway with the key role our schools play here.

Our education system now recognises the critical role that wellbeing programs play in our schools for the prevention of mental health issues. More and more schools are either looking for, or already have, a wellbeing program in place—which is great! But then how do we do this in a sustainable way so that it doesn't become the latest trend or 'fad'?

This is the same question Principal Robert Hoff asked his leadership team at Immanuel Primary School in 2012. A year later (as I was heading into my ninth year of teaching at Immanuel) the school employed, for the first time, a part-time wellbeing leader. The role was created with the aim of implementing a wellbeing strategy across the whole school. And, by their own admission, it was a challenging task because this new person was coming in with a blank canvas and with very little knowledge of how to implement such an initiative.

As the 2013 school year came to an end, nothing consistent had really stuck. You could see the odd poster on walls around the school, every so often a resource was shared and occasionally an article was emailed to staff featuring the benefit of social and emotional learning. (If you've ever worked in a corporate office, I'm sure you'll recognise the ironic similarities between this and how company values are often introduced and expected to be taken up.)

Rolling into the new school year, I knew something had to change. Cases of anxiety were on the rise at the school due to friendship issues, lack of friends, academic pressure from parents and a growing number of changing family circumstances (such as divorce).

As I was on my daily run in Glenelg East—something that I had adopted into my own routine to take care of my mental health—I took a breather, standing there on a corner, washed over in adrenaline driven by passion and I said to myself, *What if I combine what I know as a teacher with what I've learned for my own benefit in the space of positive psychology? Maybe I could not only help Immanuel Primary, but also a number of other schools implement their positive education programs.*

You see, just like we learn to ride a bike, run or play a sport or musical instrument, we can learn and practise to be a more resilient and happier person—no matter our age, gender or background.

The skills themselves—such as gratitude, kindness, empathy, positive reflection, self-awareness and serving others—are not really anything new. You might even roll your eyes when you read this and think, *Yeah, we've tried that before.* For example, maybe you've already experimented with gratitude journaling, yet 12 months later you're at the same point and still struggling to keep on top of all the anxiety, bullying and behavioural issues.

You see, the real trick is to know and understand how to teach and apply these skills in a way that works for the people you're working with: our youngest and brightest minds. We may have made a great start, but we're stuck treating instead of preventing. And we don't realise that half the time our kids find this stuff boring, so it loses its desired benefit and then, of course, it's not going to stick!

With this rush of adrenaline, I upped the pace to one that Cliff Young would give the nod to, and swiftly ran the remaining 300 metres home. I immediately started researching 'How to teach gratitude to young people' and jotted down lesson ideas. And that was the start.

Since this moment in January 2014, I have been obsessed with and have dedicated a large part of my life to creating resources and a framework to help schools and teachers with *how* to integrate positive education in the classroom and across the whole school.

As a result of starting this passion project, Growing with Gratitude (GWG) was formed. The purpose of GWG is to help schools implement wellbeing programs as well as in-person student and teacher workshops and online programs. We have created a stack of activities, games, lessons and other resources to help schools integrate their wellbeing across the school, in the classroom and at home.

It's also important to note that schools, individuals and families are at different stages in their wellbeing journeys. Some schools have invested hundreds of thousands into their wellbeing journey, some may have started but are looking for new ideas and some are just starting out. Wherever you and your school are at, there's something in this book for you.

The work we've done in schools has impacted close to half a million students and helped more than 800 schools, and it has been accessed in 45 countries. We've helped teachers, wellbeing educators and others integrate daily and weekly routines in the classroom and across the whole school.

We've tried, practised and researched the numerous activities, lessons and games shared in this book, which will help you practise the skills of resilience needed for long-term consistency across different ages.

So, everything you'll read in this book is real, practical, actionable and, most importantly, achievable. It's an accumulation of my experience and decades of working with academics, wellbeing leaders, school leaders, families, carers and the students themselves to create fun and engaging resources, frameworks and systems.

I understand that teaching is a tough job and we know a lot is added to the curriculum and little taken away. I know this because I've been there and I get it. However, I'm also aware that you know the importance of teaching wellbeing skills to students, of helping the next generation of young people grow up in a culture that promotes gratitude, happiness and resilience so they can cope, no matter what.

Whether you've been on a positive education journey for some time, only recently started, are exploring the idea or if you are a curious parent or caregiver who'd love to develop a culture of gratitude at home, this is the book for you. It is your toolkit: a guide on how you can create a culture of gratitude in your classroom, around your whole school and in your home.

What if, in 15 years' time, we look back and see a decrease in mental health issues? In bullying? In anxiety? In self-harm? The only way this is possible is if we reset and teach young people skills as early as possible that will assist them in dealing with challenges: skills that help them be adaptable thinkers, be self-aware and take ownership. I'm not saying by any means it will wipe out mental health issues altogether. As we know, mental health is very complicated, with many layers. But what we also know is the early years are critical in the development of a young person's brain, as well as for forming habits and skill development.

Today more than ever we need to stop just analysing the data and make things happen.

Now it's time to act and take the steps to implement a wellbeing or positive education curriculum across your school so that, together, we can equip the next generation with the skills they need to help them move forward through whatever life throws at them.

There's no time to waste.

Ash

HOW TO USE THIS BOOK

You can't expect to master your tennis serve the first time you practise it, and the same goes for the skills you're about to learn—and learn to implement—in this book.

This is why everything you're about to read has been designed for you to add to your own practical toolkit: one that you can keep drawing on over time. Within these pages, you'll find activities, games and ideas that you can adopt and experiment with in the classroom, across your whole school and also, importantly, at home. There are plenty of real case stories to show you how others have done the same. You'll even pick up some things you can adapt and practise in your workplace!

My suggestion for working through this book is to keep it simple and achievable. You don't need to wait until everything is perfect to start your wellbeing practice. Simply add to what you're already doing in the classroom and across your school, and expand from there.

Ideas are great, but they mean nothing without execution. So, I encourage you to choose a couple of things that resonate with you as you read, and start to action them immediately.

As you're about to see, positive education means we need to all be working together. Our future, and the future health of our next generation, depend on it.

It's also a good idea to share what you learn from this book with others, perhaps in a dedicated staff meeting, so you can start to work out ways to implement the bigger and more consistent concepts together.

You can download my free Resource Pack of all the games and activities in this book—and much more—from book.growingwithgratitude.com.au.

Keep this Resource Pack handy to draw on whenever you need—for example, when you have a spare few minutes to throw in a game before class ends or lunch begins.

Let's get into it!

CHAPTER 1
Why Growing with Gratitude?

I grew up in a sports-mad family. We had a table-tennis table set up in our parachute-lined-ceiling shed in Happy Valley, a southern suburb of Adelaide, and I loved to play with my mum Bev, dad Mark and sister Toni. We'd have a hit and then crouch around our little TV to watch sport: usually footy, cricket or basketball.

One time, I remember our family was a little nervous in the lead-up to the semifinals of the women's basketball at the Olympics in Seoul, South Korea. Australia was about to play Yugoslavia. A win would see Australia play off for a gold medal for the very first time. The reason for the butterflies was because my aunty, Pat Mickan, was playing in the game. I was only nine at the time but I understood the significance of the match and knew what it meant to my Aunty Pat, as well as all of us.

It was one of the all-time greatest Olympic basketball matches. With only seconds to go on the clock, Australia was up by one point: on the verge of making history and advancing to the gold-medal game. However, Yugoslavia had possession. With seconds to go, a Yugoslavian player threw up a shot from near the baseline. It was like slow motion watching that ball travel through the air. And damn, that ball went through the net. Australia heartbreakingly went down by a solitary point. I recall being totally devasted and in tears for Aunty Pat.

Growing up in this kind of environment, a love of sport eventually transferred over to me. I was obsessed with making it as a professional sports person. Especially given my Uncle Mark (Mum's brother) was also someone I idolised and looked up to (we all know how important those role models are). Mark was the first-ever captain of the Brisbane Bears when they first joined what was then the VFL in 1987. When the Adelaide Crows joined the AFL in 1991, Mark returned to Adelaide and was the inaugural club champion of the Adelaide Crows. He was also a SANFL premiership coach and represented South Australia in state of origin football at its peak.

In my teenage years, I excelled at cricket and Australian Rules football. I played in the As in the South Australian Grade Cricket Competition representing Southern Districts as a 15-year-old (one of the youngest ever), represented South Australia in two national under-17 championships and I had the privilege of captaining the team the second time around. Our team made the final that year and played on the hallowed turf of the MCG, but was narrowly defeated by Queensland.

At the same time, I was tracking well with football. I was in the South Australian under-18 squad which is an important pathway to playing in the AFL, and was playing good football at South Adelaide. But the demands of playing two sports started to overlap, so I felt I needed to decide: football or cricket? I chose football.

What happened next is significant to what I do today, and why.

It came to a time where there's a short window of a couple of years to impress AFL recruiters, as well as make the under-18 state team, which normally represents the top talent pool from each state. I made the South Australian squad as a 15-year-old in 1994, in 1995 and again in 1996. However, something went wrong. I never made the final team and was named as reserve in the final two years.

I managed to convince myself at the age of 17 that my AFL dream was over.

I'd mope around the house and at school with the hope that family and friends would give me the attention I was seeking. This behaviour caused self-inflicted depression. It wasn't medically diagnosed, but looking back on it, I believe I had symptoms of depression over that period. Not making it in the final year of eligibility made me believe it was over, when in reality that wasn't necessarily true.

So, what happened?

If you'd asked me back then, I would have blamed coaches, circumstances and anything else I could think of. Ask me today and it's a totally different answer.

On reflection, I realised I had the kicking, handballing and marking skills, along with the fitness (physical skills), but what was lacking was the mental fitness (the ability to handle the mental challenges of sport and life). I realise now, I wasn't equipped with the skills needed to be a resilient person.

Don't you wish you'd been taught the skills to manage these ups and downs, setbacks and failures back then, so you could weather any kind of storm now?

I'm sure as an adult, you can recall a similar story from your past.

How did you handle it then? How would you handle it now?

Don't you wish you'd been taught the skills to manage these ups and downs, setbacks and failures back then, so you could weather any kind of storm now?

How would your life be different if you were taught skills from as young as four or five years that helped deal with all kinds of challenges?

A different kind of value

From a young age, we learn that society values physical performance and academic success. However, I feel my story, and no doubt one of yours, is why we need to focus more on the softer skills—such as resilience.

In reality, our greatest learnings come from taking risks, moving forward from challenges, being adaptable thinkers and learning from the experiences that let us down.

Back then, I didn't have the skills to move forward from poor performance or reframe situations when things didn't go my way. I lacked self-awareness and rarely took ownership. I also took for granted a number of things, such as having the opportunity to play, the equipment and facilities, the coaches and volunteers. I put so much pressure on myself that I forgot why I originally started to play sport when I was five and that was to have fun playing with my mates!

Thankfully, in low times I never popped pills to manage; instead I popped gratitude, physical activity, empathy, kindness, positive reflection, service and self-awareness. It is these skills that I believe get me through life as an adult and formed the basis for my company, Growing with Gratitude.

Without a doubt, we've come a long way in our education system since I was at school and we've recognised the need for skills that work on our mental health.

Think about what kinds of things you currently do at school (and, I bet, never did back then!). Maybe you've had some form of staff training, the school has recommended or is using wellbeing resources or perhaps has invested in a wellbeing program for its teachers to use, such as Growing with Gratitude or another program to help build your students' emotional capacity. And, if you're lucky, a wellbeing lesson has been added into the timetable.

Yet unfortunately, while many of us have made a great start on these skills, we still report a lot of it feels hit and miss. How do we know this? Mental health is still on the rise, and bullying is at an all-time high.

So, what's going wrong?

Three key challenges

It's likely that right now some of you ensure wellbeing is included in your daily and weekly timetable, others do a wellbeing lesson every so often and then there's a small percentage of you who don't (yet) do any wellbeing at all. Why?

A lot of our wellbeing initiatives are seen as add-ons to everything else we're doing. As a consequence, we're not implementing them or driving them in the right way. I have come across too many schools to count where they start their wellbeing programs out strong and then after a term or two they fizzle out. Many schools have this haphazard approach and it's hard to get things going or make them stick.

From my observations over the past decade, a pattern of challenges has formed:

1. *We're treating problems, not preventing them.* What if we taught young people how to build relationships and how to be great friends from an early age? Would bullying be the major issue that it is today?

A 2018 study by the Make Bullying History Foundation reported 80 per cent of students believe bullying is a serious problem at their school and what is even more alarming is that 59 per cent of students said they've experienced bullying. Cyber bullying and online bullying have played a major role in causing such high rates.

Teaching positive friendships alongside empathy could possibly be the prevention strategy we're looking for to reduce bullying. Research from Salavera and colleagues concludes that:

> ... *teachers and other members of the school community should work on empathy with young people from an early age, in order to help students and reduce bullying in the classroom.*

My friend and colleague Dana Kerford is founder of URSTRONG, an organisation built around empowering others with friendship skills. Dana shares that 'relationships are at the heart of wellbeing. Learning how to create healthy friendships and manage conflict in a respectful way is the key to creating cultures of kindness in schools'.

2. *We only have one person 'in charge' of wellbeing.* And this is often handballed to them! Maybe it's the wellbeing leader, whose role it is to oversee the wellbeing program. That means they are often pulled every which way, including spending time on those behaviour-management issues.

3. *We're time poor.* Let's face it: we're just too busy with—you know—teaching! So, when we do finally 'make time' we are using ineffective strategies, so it feels much harder than it is, and our kids are not getting any real benefit.

It's important to know that none of this is your fault. We don't need to play the blame game here.

Yes, we may be time poor, but there are ways to prioritise wellbeing and to fit it in, in ways you may not have thought of. Granted, there will be issues that come up, that require reactive action; therefore a solid pastoral care structure is important. However, a wellbeing program is a long-term approach to preventing problems by teaching young people skills to help deal with challenges, and to build friendships and a sense of belonging. So, it's unfair and unrealistic to think wellbeing is *one* person's responsibility when in fact it's everyone's.

There's no doubt teachers and the school play a key role in setting up a strong wellbeing environment; however, it's important to note they are not solely responsible for the wellbeing of students. The home plays a key role too. A lot of wellbeing initiatives can be transferred between school and home, and (as you're about to see) the things we practise in the classroom can be practised around the dinner table, in the car or other times you are with your kids.

It's also important to note that, unfortunately, some students may not receive the nurturing they need in their home life; therefore, school could be the only place where they will receive wellbeing practice—that's why a **We can grow our schools and homes with gratitude and other skills that will set our kids up for life.** good start is needed. (And some individual students may need professional help outside of what a school can provide.)

We can grow our schools and homes with gratitude and other skills that will set our kids up for life.

A shift in mindset is vital in integrating a strong, robust and effective positive education program in the classroom and across the whole school, to avoid the 'half-arsed' approach currently being used.

An invitation to come together

The schools already doing amazing work in this space are few and far between. We need to get every school up to scratch!

The information in this book will help close that gap.

I will share with you how to grow with gratitude in your classrooms, across your whole school, at home and in your personal life, too (because you simply can't look after others unless you're looking after yourself first).

Don't just take my word for it.

One of the people I most respect is recently retired Principal Robert Hoff who has 50 years' experience in education. He was an early adopter when it came to wellbeing practices and a whole-school approach. In a recent interview with me, he said:

> If the COVID pandemic has taught us anything, it is that all of us are in this together! Our own and other people's wellbeing is clearly in each individual's hands. It is the civic responsibility of each person to care for themselves, their own family, school acquaintances and community members. Never in our lifetime has it been so clear that our own action or inaction has a critical path to play in our and others' wellbeing.
>
> We probably knew this before with the spread of the influenza virus (and its impact on school health) but it may have been moved to the back of our minds. In recent decades, research has clearly demonstrated that the wellbeing of students depends so much on the spirit of the school. Who is responsible for creating a flourishing school environment? Simple answer: staff, students, parents and school council members are the leaders. There are others, such as grandparents and coaches, but, essentially, it's up to those listed above.
>
> Staff, particularly those who have daily contact with students, have the key role. It is essential that staff have the latest

research about what creates a positive school environment where students can flourish.

Significant and continuing growth by staff is absolutely essential. Everyone needs to understand why wellbeing is the priority for every school. One of the first areas to explore is the factors that lead to teachers' own personal wellbeing. Once this is achieved, then 'buy in to "wellbeing for all"' has a significant chance of success.

Educators need to understand their own personal wellbeing and the factors that create a stable, fulfilled and flourishing life. Few are flourishing in top gear all of the time. We are not running on all pistons emotionally, physically and spiritually all of the time. But we all do strive to be resilient, reliable, effective and confident most of the time.

Dealing with the daily action of school life can be testing indeed. Why do some thrive and others just survive? I am certain that if educators embed key aspects of wellbeing into their own living, and, indeed, continue to grow in the understanding of what contributes to their own wellbeing, then they will more easily share these essential skills with young people under their care.

When staff discovered the science of positive psychology through a carefully managed process of activities that focus on what makes a life most worthwhile, developing positive individual characteristics, they began to realise their strengths and that passing on their values matter.

They find it stimulating learning about the fundamental tools of developing a flourishing life for themselves and how their contribution to the life of students and the school really matters. This wouldn't have happened if the leadership team had left this to chance.

On that note, it's important to highlight that I am not a mental health professional, psychologist or qualified counsellor, nor have I ever claimed to be. What I am, though, is a passionate educator with over 20 years' experience who is obsessed with figuring out the best approaches to wellbeing in classrooms, schools and at home.

What you're about to read—the journey we are about to embark on—is based on my personal and professional experience over that time. I've sought out the best case studies, interviews, stories and examples, so that you don't just learn from me, but also from each other!

It's now up to us to take the next step, together.

To put things into practice, I'll ask you to try, do or action something from each chapter after you've read it. And of course, you can download the accompanying resource pack to help you.

It's now up to us to take the next step, together.

NOW FOR ACTION
Be a role model for growing with gratitude

We can never underestimate the value of role models in our lives and you are a role model in the life of the young people in your care.

Consider your own wellbeing. What is one thing you do to maintain/increase your wellbeing (e.g. exercise, meditation, playing with pets)?

Share with your class/child what you do to increase your wellbeing or improve your mood.

This type of role modelling may just encourage our young people to give growing with gratitude a go. And you never know, it may be life changing for them.

CHAPTER 2
Embed commitment

In 2020, Mark Butler, a fantastic educator from Ireland, became principal of Al Durrah International School in Sharjah, UAE. At this time, a sequence of events occurred that led the school to decide that a strong wellbeing program was needed. Mark explains:

Society and family pressures had students fixated on grades. It is quite common for students to have this obsession with receiving 90 per cent average grades because the students have a significant chance of receiving scholarships.

So, the focus is on getting As and A+s and it got to the point where they'd do anything to get those grades, which at the time included plagiarism issues.

He could see the stressful impact this was having on students and staff. This was the tipping point that led Mark to realise things needed to change. Mark kindly shares:

It was around this time, that I came across Ash's LinkedIn and I noticed the content he was sharing on gratitude, self-reflection, resilience and other similar positive habits. So, we committed to using some of his resources.

Historically, it was believed wellbeing wasn't everyone's responsibility—it was just one person's—so Mark had to change this perception and teach the staff that it's actually everyone's job. Mark shares:

Staff had a very poor understanding of wellbeing; they've never really been involved in any type of dialogue around wellbeing. There was only one person in the school who had a good understanding and he was trying to drive it on his own. Therefore, I had to start off by breaking it down, like 'What is wellbeing?' I started with trainings. I trained the kindergarten team, primary team and secondary teams. All staff were included.

Being committed is one of the most important steps to embedding a strong positive education program across your school — and this relies on everyone in the whole school being involved.

The staff's attitude to wellbeing—that it was the responsibility of the lone wellbeing leader—wasn't their fault. They simply weren't aware of the role they could play in the wellbeing of students, as well as in supporting each other. This is when Mark made the decision that he needed to educate his staff in the importance of wellbeing and show them how to integrate wellbeing into the classroom and across the school.

Being committed is one of the most important steps to embedding a strong positive education program across your school—and this relies on everyone in the whole school being involved.

That's what commitment is about.

A whole-school approach

First and foremost, school leaders and staff need to be committed to embedding wellbeing across the whole school. This may seem obvious, but it's often overlooked. When you dive a little deeper, the commitment is only verbal, with very little action being taken to ensure a strong program is in place. On other occasions, schools start out like a bull at a gate—train staff, implement some practices—and then a few months later it's all come to a halt.

So, the first question you have to ask to ensure this doesn't happen to you is 'What is it that everyone thinks they are committing to?'

I was speaking to a brilliant educator from Melbourne recently who was super excited about commencing her new position as wellbeing leader. In fact, when I reached out to ask her a question in regards to this book, she told me she had resigned from the role because the school's view on wellbeing didn't align with hers. In her words:

My role ended up being behaviour management and student welfare, which is definitely not a preventative model. My idea was more about wellbeing in general, such as running resilience and wellbeing programs and supporting the school overall in that way.

That story shows that 'wellbeing' is a broad topic and it may have a different meaning for different people. It's important to be clear on what you are committing to so that you are consistent across the board.

I am a huge fan of the definition that Scotch College in Adelaide has embraced. It's from Dr Rachel Dodge:

In essence, stable wellbeing is when individuals have the psychological, social and physical resources they need to meet a particular psychological, social and/or physical challenge. When individuals have more challenges than resources, the see-saw dips, along with their wellbeing, and vice-versa.

Shawn Kasbergen, Director of Student Wellbeing at Scotch explains:

> ...*this definition gives the implication that wellbeing is always in a state of flux. If we perceive that there are too many challenges for the resources we possess, our wellbeing can decline. Conversely, if we don't experience adequate challenge in our lives, individuals can stagnate and lack a sense of meaning and purpose.*

So, commitment to wellbeing is not only helping students, but also staff build their toolkits to help deal with psychological, social and physical challenges that could arise in this ever-changing world.

This is the preventative approach we must commit to. I like to call this building and protecting wellbeing. You are also committing to the implementation by taking action in the classroom and across the whole school (and if you're a parent, you may consider committing to implementing this at home).

Not one, but all

Just as Mark Butler did at Al Durrah, any program will be most effective when everyone is on the same page.

Remember, it's unrealistic and unfair to think it's one person's responsibility, when in fact it's everyone's.

The real issue is, you've probably noticed that some teachers are keen to take on school initiatives, such as wellbeing, and other staff don't like change/new things being introduced and will therefore be resistant.

This issue can be explained using the diffusion of innovation theory, as shown in figure 2.1.

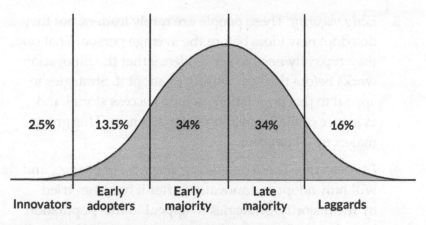

| 2.5% | 13.5% | 34% | 34% | 16% |

Innovators | Early adopters | Early majority | Late majority | Laggards

Figure 2.1: Diffusion of innovation theory

American sociologist Everett Rogers created the theory based on the fact that innovations are not adopted by all individuals in a social system over the same time sequence. The theory can be classified into five adopter categories according to how long it takes each group to begin using the new idea.

The five adopter categories, as outlined by Wayne LaMorte from Boston University School of Public Health, are:

1. *Innovators:* These are people who want to be the first to try the innovation. They are venturesome and interested in new ideas. These people are very willing to take risks, and are often the first to develop new ideas. Very little, if anything, needs to be done to appeal to this population. They make up 2.5 per cent.

2. *Early adopters:* These are people who represent opinion leaders. They enjoy leadership roles, and embrace change opportunities. They are already aware of the need to change and so are very comfortable adopting new ideas. Strategies to appeal to this population include how-to manuals and information sheets on implementation. They do not need information to convince them to change. They make up 13.5 per cent.

3. *Early majority*: These people are rarely leaders, but they do adopt new ideas before the average person. That said, they typically need to see evidence that the innovation works before they are willing to adopt it. Strategies to appeal to this population include success stories and evidence of the innovation's effectiveness. This group makes up 34 per cent.

4. *Late majority*: These people are sceptical of change, and will only adopt an innovation after it has been tried by the majority. Strategies to appeal to this population include information on how many other people have tried the innovation and have adopted it successfully. Late majority make up 34 per cent.

5. *Laggards:* These people are bound by tradition and very conservative. They are very sceptical of change and are the hardest group to bring on board. Strategies to appeal to this population include statistics, fear appeals and pressure from people in the other adopter groups. These people make up 16 per cent.

What this means is that, in terms of embedding commitment in your school, you need to focus on the early adopters and early majority first to make things happen. These middle categories are typically more willing to try new things and are often the risk takers. Avoid spending your time and energy on convincing the laggards of the need for wellbeing initiatives.

Ben Catalano, principal of Tenison Woods Catholic School, is fully aware of the innovation of diffusion theory. He explains how he introduces wellbeing in the context of knowing you will have early adopters, laggards and everything in between: 'Teacher education is number one. Covering what positive education is and the basics of it'.

Avoid spending your time and energy on convincing the laggards of the need for wellbeing initiatives.

From here Ben explains:

Every time I have introduced wellbeing to a school, nearly immediately I'll have a handful of staff approach me, wanting to know more and to access resources. These are my early adopters. They are the voice for wellbeing.

Ben engages with his early adopters to help with wellbeing initiatives and to run ideas past them. He says, 'I often step back and let the early adopters take over'. The early adopters could even form part of your wellbeing advisory committee (which we will talk about shortly).

Ben also highlights the importance of consistency around messaging:

It's important as a leader to be 'vocal' about wellbeing. At my previous school [St Martin's De Porres], after two years we made it clear wellbeing is part of the school—it's not just a catch phrase.

This included updating school documents and policies to say wellbeing is part of the school culture and when a new teacher starts at the school, they are fully aware that wellbeing is at the forefront.

But what about the late majority and laggards? Ben shares: 'Some do see it as important, but perhaps they're overwhelmed and aren't prepared to embed it in their classroom to the extent we'd like'.

I love Ben's advice:

So what we say to the laggards is certain wellbeing initiatives are non-negotiable. For example, we invested in an explicitly taught curriculum/resources that we ensured were timetabled in every classroom. This was the non-negotiable: that it would be taught with the resources/scope and sequence. However, we ensured that all staff had a knowledgeable other or early adaptor as a support. This way no staff felt left behind.

Ben has found this approach extremely effective when dealing with the complexities of staff. And he also made a great point that:

> *I am so passionate about wellbeing and making it part of the school culture and there's so much evidence out there as to the benefit, I will always go in to bat for positive education, and I have so much research to point laggards towards if I need to.*

Over time everyone will see the benefit and be swayed by the adopter groups who are raving fans.

A youthful and passionate educator, Andrew Mittiga teaches at Wilderness School in Adelaide. In a fantastic wellbeing discussion over coffee he brought up the topic of change fatigue. Sara Antliff, Talent Management Lead at Atlassian, sums up change fatigue as 'resistance or passive resignation to organizational changes on the part of an employee'.

As a leader, it's important to be mindful of change fatigue and to not introduce too many new ideas all at the same time to staff.

Move your troops

Once you've got a few of your early adopters up and running, you can start to champion the others in a couple of ways.

Staff training

You will need to train *all* staff on the importance of wellbeing, its benefits, how they can execute wellbeing in the classroom and how you will do it across the whole school.

Training could occur in staff meetings and on student-free days, but it's highly recommended that you have a group of staff, or at least one member, attend an external training session and then train your staff on what they learned.

You could also bring in experts to run training and ensure you have staff action what they learn—and be sure to follow up. Too often we invest in teacher training, the motivation is there for 24 hours and then life happens and we forget to action what we learn. It's a *must* that you action what you learn.

As a wellbeing or school leader, or as a teacher, why not step up and offer to run a staff training session. It could be an idea you've come across, a resource you can share or a whole-school initiative. Just make sure you include a stack of activities and the purpose behind them to keep everyone involved and engaged.

It's a *must* that you action what you learn.

Wellbeing advisory committees

If you don't have one already, I'd highly recommend creating a wellbeing advisory committee. A strong wellbeing committee will feature the wellbeing leader, a second school leader, passionate teachers across year levels, students and parents. To take your committee to the next level, look to include a psychiatrist, psychologist or counsellor and a wellbeing expert.

The role of the committee is to:

- share passion
- listen to the student members (they'll tell you what they want on behalf of their peers)
- come up with resources to share with teachers for using in class, as well as whole-school initiatives
- develop staff training
- book outside facilitators for staff training and student in-class sessions/workshops.

Scotch College in Adelaide has recently formed its very own wellbeing advisory committee. Shawn Kasbergen explains, 'the wellbeing advisory committee is an equal representation of students, staff and community members. The group will advocate for, enable and enhance the wellbeing provision for the College community'.

The committee features teachers, students, psychiatrists, a psychologist and developmental educator, and a mindfulness advocate. The committee comes together once per term.

When considering inviting professionals and experts to your wellbeing committee, look in your school community first, as there could well be parents, grandparents or old scholars you could invite—this is an excellent way of transferring wellbeing from school to home and vice versa.

Student voice group

Have you got a student voice group, a student representative council (SRC) or governing council (your school may have a different name for student representatives) at your school? In addition to these important student groups, have you considered setting up a student wellbeing club (SWC)?

If you haven't yet established such a group, I'd highly recommend you do so as a way to help drive your whole school's approach to wellbeing.

Student voice matters. According to the Australian Research Council (ARC), students appreciate opportunities to participate meaningfully and to have an influence in school decision making and activities such as supporting higher levels of wellbeing. Furthermore, the higher the level of participation, the higher the level of student wellbeing.

You could set your student wellbeing club up in one of the following ways:

- Each year level or class has two or more representatives
- Form your club featuring students from your senior classes
- Include wellbeing into the role of an established student group, such as the SRC.

In chapter 6 we will dive deeper into student-led initiatives and why these are so important. But for now, get curious about the opportunities that are available to you and your school.

Here's a story from a real school to help.

Lessons from Hong Kong

In August 2018, Kellett School in Hong Kong committed to embed wellbeing across the school. Mark Steed, Principal and CEO, shared these five lessons learned from his team's experience:

1. *It is essential to have a culture where the wellbeing of the community has a high priority in the strategic and operational decision-making process (the commitment).*

2. *An effective wellbeing program needs resources: staffing, training, space (we have just created a dedicated meditation space) and, most importantly, that scarcest resource of all, time.*

3. *Regular monitoring of student and staff wellbeing is important. In practice it doesn't really matter whether this is done using an app or a Google form, but taking the pulse of the community and acting on the feedback has been at the heart of our approach.*

4. *Wellbeing programs do not replace the need for robust and extensive pastoral care structures. Over time, we have come to see 'Positively Kellett' [their wellbeing program] as a proactive approach to student wellbeing, whereas our pastoral structures, by necessity, need to be reactive. The wheels sometimes do fall off for students and staff and it is important that there is a team trained and ready to support them.*

5. *Wellbeing is not the sole responsibility of the school. It has to be a partnership. School leaders have a particular responsibility to create a school culture that enhances wellbeing and to allocate the (sometimes limited) resources at their disposal in a way that protects and enhances student and staff wellbeing. However, individuals need to do their part, too. Everyone needs to take a level of responsibility for their own physical and mental health, which means taking care of the basics (sleep, diet and exercise) and seeking help when times get tough.*

We'll look at more of these ideas—especially looking after yourself—later in the book. But first, in the next chapter, we'll explore how you can make time for wellbeing in specific and concrete ways.

NOW FOR ACTION
Stop and reflect

- Where do you think you and your school is at in terms of wellbeing right now?

- Is your school truly committed to wellbeing? Or is it currently 'patchy'?

- What wellbeing practices have you committed to as a whole school? As a school, do you do them well?

- Where do you think the commitment could improve?

- Do you have regular staff training?

- Do you have a wellbeing committee?

- Do you have a student voice group?

Following your reflection, consider what action you could take to ensure the crucial step of commitment is embedded.

CHAPTER 3
Allocate wellbeing time and routines

Not that long ago, I visited a primary school situated in the mid-north of South Australia. The acting principal seemed quite stressed. She explained that her principal was on leave due to a serious knee injury he suffered during a social basketball game. She was doing her best to cover the role of principal as well as her usual role as wellbeing leader.

I asked, 'How are you fitting in wellbeing at the moment?' I found her response interesting, yet alarming at the same time.

She explained, 'Well we are in the process of making wellbeing part of our health lessons. When our principal returns, I will take a lesson a week for each class'.

I then asked, 'How have you allocated the time for wellbeing in the past?' She said they usually 'leave it up to the teachers to include in class time, but those teachers are busier and overloaded like we've never seen before'.

When prompted as to why she thought this was, she responded immediately:

Data collection. Everyone wants data. The government want data, particularly around literacy and numeracy, and this is taking up a lot of teacher time. Our most experienced teachers, who have been teaching for 25-plus years, say they haven't been this busy in all their time.

Not surprisingly, there is a lot of emphasis on literacy and numeracy skills (which, of course, are absolutely important) and wellbeing is then forgotten. And as we know, wellbeing can be hard to measure. Yet, the skills of wellbeing are crucial to being able to manage life these days—not to mention all the literacy and numeracy tests and assessments!

So, *how do we allocate the time in our classrooms and across the school for wellbeing?* It's a key point because many components of wellbeing are skills that need cultivating, and we need time so that students can practise.

Just like learning and practising sport skills, learning a language or going to the gym to improve our fitness, we need to allocate time to prioritise and practise wellbeing.

It's time for wellbeing

What's the vibe around your staffroom when the commitment is made to integrate something new, such as wellbeing, into the curriculum?

I'm tipping it's met with mixed reactions. The teachers who already understand the benefits of wellbeing and are probably already implementing elements of positive education in the classroom are super excited. Then there are those who won't say much at all and are happy to go with the flow. And there are those who make comments such as, 'Here's another thing we have to do; how are we going to fit this into an already packed timetable?'

It's pretty much the diffusion of innovation theory (which we discussed in chapter 2) in action. Varying reactions are common and that's 100 per cent understandable. We are all already so super busy and this, in essence, is the problem. There's already the day-to-day pressures of school life, such as lesson planning, assessment, behaviour management and parent expectations, and then there are always 'things' being added, such as increased data collection requirements. Add to that dealing with students who lack effort, are disrespectful and are even sometimes aggressive. Top it all off with your own busy home life—that's quite a lot of pressure!

So, to allow for a strong, robust wellbeing program, we have to *all* make time for wellbeing—not for it to be seen as a thing you simply 'fit in'. This is *not* about putting more pressure on teachers to include wellbeing into other subject areas or squeezing it into an already jam-packed curriculum.

This is *not* about putting more pressure on teachers to include wellbeing into other subject areas or squeezing it into an already jam-packed curriculum.

I have come across schools where they say they're committed, yet they leave it up to the teachers to include wellbeing in the already full curriculum. This is what makes the wellbeing program 'patchy'. It's a huge weight off a teacher's shoulders when that lesson time is set and they can focus on providing students with quality lessons to practise.

Once we allocate the time using our whole-school approach, research from the Association of Independent Schools of NSW informs us wellbeing interventions are effective overall for improving key aspects of wellbeing, including social-emotional-learning skill development, positive attitudes and social behaviours, fewer conduct problems, less emotional distress and better academic performance.

Whole-school interventions have been shown to improve wellbeing, reduce internalising problems and support gains in interpersonal and intrapersonal attitudes and skills. This provides strong evidence for the overall effectiveness of school-based interventions to support student wellbeing.

This is why we must *all* allocate the time for wellbeing. In fact, Principal Mark Butler at Al Durrah International School reported that embedding wellbeing into the timetable has seen less student referrals to the social and emotional counsellor. He's also found that it's far easier to coordinate, monitor, observe and evaluate the school's approach to wellbeing. This is why we must *all* allocate the time for wellbeing.

Examples of wellbeing at work

The best way to demonstrate how we can allocate the right time for wellbeing is to see it in action. So, let's look at a couple of quick examples to show what that looks like in practice, not just theory. You'll also notice that some of these examples show how we can integrate wellbeing between school and home.

Example 1: Al Durrah International School

At Al Durrah, Mark Butler made a concerted effort to train all of his staff so they understood the importance of including positive education into the timetable. Mark explains:

We understood, to have a truly impactful, positive education program we had to make some changes to the schedule to make it happen. We included a dedicated lesson for wellbeing by shortening recess and lunchtime breaks by five minutes, and we shortened all lesson times by five minutes. This enabled us to go from six lessons to seven lessons a day.

To get the all-clear, Mark took the proposal to the governing council, which approved it. So, in this case, the school shortened break and lesson times to turn a six-lesson timetable into seven lessons, enabling daily wellbeing. A win for everyone!

Example 2: Prince of Peace Lutheran School

In Brisbane, the Prince of Peace Lutheran School allocated a wellbeing lesson every Friday. The leadership team allowed the teachers to choose when to run the session, according to what best suited the needs of their class.

They also incorporated wellbeing in their home learning. Head of Junior Campus Anne-Marie Schmidt explains:

Prince of Peace uses wellbeing tasks as part of homework, often depending on what the year level focus is. As a school that still gives homework, there is maths, spelling, reading and wellbeing. Sometimes students do 'home service' (helping out around home, as a way to practise serving others) and we highlight in our assemblies what home service students have completed. Families send in pictures and share stories of their children doing home service. We share and highlight this skill.

During COVID-19 lockdowns, Prince of Peace had a major focus on wellbeing home-learning tasks. Anne-Marie shares:

We set wellbeing tasks extensively during home learning in COVID-19 times. Our teachers took the lead and organised this and it helped students redirect their thoughts to more positive things during the height of the pandemic, which was really appreciated by our families.

Setting wellbeing tasks and activities as homework is an awesome, but often under-utilised, way to practise wellbeing. As Anne-Marie pointed out: it's one more way to practise. Another benefit is, it helps families to use the same language around wellbeing as the students do at school, creating a consistent approach at home and school.

Example 3: JBCN International School, Oshiwara

In Mumbai, India, the JBCN International School allocates one lesson a week to wellbeing, as well as including it as part of its daily morning routines. The weekly session is known as the 'optimism period'. This lesson occurs across all year levels from K–12. What they learn depends on their year level.

Vice Principal Ana Dominguez explains:

In the optimism lesson time topics range from how to deal with failure, and the importance of failure, to body image, to peer pressure, how to handle bullying and feeling well in general…

In our primary grades, we have additional 'quality circle time' every day. Students have the opportunity to voice their feelings and share their positive emotions. For example, what they are looking forward to in their day, how they are going to work as a team, empathy and compassion for others as well as expressing gratitude.

The school is brilliant at making *everyone* feel like they belong. Ana shares: 'Our students are amazing at recognising and showing gratitude to cleaners, security and other staff. This makes everyone feel they belong'.

And another example of making students feel they belong is that all staff know the names of *all* students. Yep, I couldn't believe it either. And, this is not a small school!

In addition, the secondary students have 10 minutes available in the morning, prior to their first lesson. One of the activities they do in this time is take it in turns to share an inspirational quote they have discovered. Ana elaborates, 'They discuss the quote and it's really about bringing a positive vibe to the day'. They also use this 10 minutes to discuss class matters.

Additionally, they've allocated time after school, which is student driven. In fact, it was created by an individual student. It's called the Anvil. The purpose is to discuss mental wellbeing issues and how to overcome them. Approximately 20 students attend each session. (When asked, Ana didn't know why it was called the Anvil. I guess it's the students being creative and combining a metalworking tool with wellbeing.)

Example 4: Faith Lutheran, Plainland

This year 7–12 school in rural Queensland has adopted an innovative 'Wednesday Program' that focuses on the holistic attributes of contemporary education, including dedicated time for student wellbeing. The program features no formal academic subjects, but instead utilises other activities to build life skills and attributes that assist with, and enhance, the students' abilities to learn—acknowledging that overall wellbeing and relationship-based approaches to teaching and learning are key drivers of academic success.

Director of Learning Communities at the school, Mr Reid Dobson, explains further:

The idea for the Wednesday Program originally came from a desire to reignite students' love for learning. When schools look to implement a positive psychology or wellbeing framework, it is usually restricted to short 'bursts' or sporadic, disconnected activities. There may be an hour one day, 15 minutes on other days, with no flow or consistency.

However, Faith Lutheran have gone down a different path. Reid continues:

We mapped it out so that, in addition to our daily wellbeing and positive psychology practices, there is a defined time in the structure of the week where we can proactively link holistic wellbeing—which includes social, emotional, physical, mental and spiritual components—to the overall student outcomes we want for each individual student. Our Wednesdays include small-group mentoring, known as 'Learning Coach', where students have the opportunity to discuss work with their teachers, perform community and relationship-building activities and exercises focused on character strengths, and use a tool called 'Pulse' to check in and track their overall wellbeing.

During the day, students are also presented with an opportunity to engage in their own passion projects, which don't necessarily align with traditional academic subjects, but allow for self-motivated exploration of topics and development of skills through project-based learning. Some of these projects include learning sign language, producing podcasts, entrepreneurial construction projects and learning to canoe on the Brisbane River. Students are also encouraged to consider utilising this time to focus on student-led initiatives across the community, allowing for self-instigated development in areas such as social consciousness, altruism and global citizenship. This is a brilliant example of allocating time to wellbeing.

Example 5: Canadian International School, Singapore

Jamila MacArthur took up her role as Head of Student Support and Wellbeing at Canadian International School (CIS) at the beginning of the 2021/2022 school year. One of the first things she introduced was 'Strong Starts'.

Grade 4 teacher Alison Jamieson shares:

We do our Strong Starts in the first 10–15 minutes to help students have a strong start to the day. They include Purposeful Partnering—that helps students strengthen their relationships, breathing to help students be mindful and then goal setting, where students set themselves a goal for the day.

Alison has also witnessed the benefit of the daily Strong Starts. She explains:

We had a busy day Tuesday and I asked the students if they were okay with skipping the Strong Start? One student responded with, 'I feel like I need this, so that I can focus on my writing', another student said 'I feel like I really need this today'. It is so nice to see that students are recognizing the benefits of taking time for their wellness and how it makes them feel.

Grade 3 teacher Jessica Hertz also shares the powerful impact the 'Strong Starts' have had on her class:

The routine of it (Strong Starts), the joy and smiles to begin the learning has brought us together as a fabulous little learning community. I have never had a group of kids who if I partner them up with anyone, they gel and collaborate. I attribute that to the Strong Starts. We have now started using the Growing with Gratitude wheel for our Purposeful Partnering and the kids LOVE it.

The class teachers have also found other ways to allocate time to wellbeing across the week and as part of daily routines. Alison explains:

We do Monday Check-ins through Google Forms. I ask 3 or 4 questions like: what was the best part of the weekend? How are you feeling today? How are you feeling about a specific assignment? Is there anything I can do to support you? Who is a friend that makes you happy? And is there something you think I need to know to help you learn?

Alison has been amazed at what they are willing to share and it's a quick way to find out how her students are feeling and what they are thinking. She also shares:

We have turned it into a Guess Who game at times where I read out what they did for the weekend and the classmates guess who it was. It is a nice way to help build community. They actually ask to play this every week now.

Recognising that immediately after breaks can be an effective time for wellbeing, CIS schedules 'calm time' after recess. During this 10-minute time the lights are dimmed, calm music is played and relaxing visuals are shown on screen, giving students a chance to find a personal space. Alison elaborates:

The students practice deep breathing, draw, read, stretch, put their head on the desk and rest and even call a chat to solve a problem with a friend in the hall. The students have shared how they appreciate having the time to calm down both physically and emotionally to get ready to focus.

Allocating the first 10–15 minutes of the day to wellbeing time, as well as finding those short moments across your day and week, is a simple, yet highly impactful, way of setting up a strong, consistent wellbeing program at your school. And as Jessica and Alison mentioned, the students look forward to it and love it.

Example 6: Berri Regional Secondary College

Berri Regional Secondary College in South Australia has recently extended its morning home room time by 30 minutes. This time is used for wellbeing and relationship building.

Donna Safralidis, Assistant Principal and Wellbeing and Engagement Leader, says they offer an elective subject called Health & Wellbeing at years 9 and 10 and then also at stages 1 (year 11) and 2 (year 12) Health.

The school's year-10 co-ordinator, Michael Toogood, explains:

Our elective subjects are currently four, one-hour lessons per week. We offer quite a few different electives including Health and Wellbeing, Outdoor Ed, Woodwork, Metalwork, Digi Tech, Business and Enterprise, and Food Tech.

With all the elective options available, it's interesting and fantastic to see close to 40 per cent of students choose to do the Health and Wellbeing elective.

Year 7 and 8 students also participate in passion projects every Friday for 90 minutes. Donna elaborates:

At the start of the school year teachers pitch a passion of theirs to the students. The students then choose the project that they are most interested in pursuing. There are approximately 15 to choose from, including connecting to community through volunteering, CrossFit, flip cameras and STEM building as examples. We've seen this form of wellbeing time being highly impactful for students because they are able to connect with like-minded students and staff. Students are also better engaged in learning because they have chosen their focus and are keen to build skills. Attendance for this cohort is 4 per cent higher on the days that students engage in their passion projects.

Wellbeing at home and in class

As you have hopefully picked up from the previous examples, working on wellbeing in your own school can be a lot simpler than you first think.

For example, allocating the first few minutes of the day to a short wellbeing activity is a fantastic way to kick off the day on a positive note. This can be part of your morning routine by having the activity instructions visible on the whiteboard or smartboard, so as soon as the students enter the class, they know they need to complete the task. Alternatively, you could allow students to settle, take the roll and then jump into the short activity altogether.

Then there's always the wrap-up to a lesson or day. If students finish their work early, there is nothing stopping you from running a wellbeing game for the last 10 minutes. Having games and activities on hand for them to engage in is a highly valuable use of time for those students who tend to work faster.

These same routines are highly effective when learning from home, so you can easily run this as a parent or if you're ever isolated at home. In addition, when school is in full swing you could allocate time in the morning or evening as part of your routine; for example, in the morning while having breakfast, around the dinner table in the evening or, on those super busy days, in the car between commitments.

I'll share more activities and games in detail in chapter 5, but a good example of an activity that is quick and effective to do in any of these scenarios is Lucky Dip Gratitude. This is also one you can play with your children at home if you are a parent.

OVER TO YOU
Lucky Dip Gratitude

Lucky Dip Gratitude is an all-time favourite activity that creates mystery and anticipation. The game is a fun way to practise gratitude and other positive habits. It can be played as part of your morning routine, as a brain break or extended into a longer game.

You will need:

- a container, jar or bowl
- the Lucky Dip questions (see figure 3.1), individually written on paper and cut out. (These are also provided in the downloadable Resource Pack.)

Lucky dip questions

What have you got coming up that you are looking forward to?

Who is a person in your life you are grateful for and why?

Describe something that you do often that makes you happy and say why.

Describe something kind you could do for someone and at some stage today do it.

What do you appreciate about your teacher and why?

What is an act of kindness someone did for you recently and how did you feel?

What is an opportunity you have had that you are grateful for?

What do you get excited about and why?

What are you doing when you are at your happiest?

What is something you could do to help out at home today? Be sure to do it.

Describe something you are particularly grateful for in your life.

Look around the room. What is something you can see that you are grateful for and why?

What has been the best part of your day so far and why?

Who is a person in your life you are grateful for and why?

What is something that made you laugh recently?

If you are feeling sad, what do you do to make yourself feel better?

What is a strength of yours and why do you think it's a strength?

What is your favourite fitness activity and why?

Who is a person you look up to and why?

Figure 3.1: Lucky Dip questions

(continued)

How to play:

1. Place the slips of paper featuring the questions in a bowl, container or jar.

2. Player 1 dips their hand in the container and pulls out a question relating to gratitude, kindness, positive reflection, and so on.

3. Player 1 reads out the question or, as the game leader, you could read out the question.

4. Player 1 responds by answering the question.

5. Once player 1 has responded, repeat the process until every player has had a turn.

Variations:

- Choose only one player to dip their hand in the container and pull out a question. Write the question on the board and have all players write down their responses individually or in pairs. Players share their responses with the class.

- Have all players seated with a note pad and pencil. Move around the room and have each player dip their hand into the container and pull out a question. Each player responds to their question by writing their response on their note pad. You could repeat this process a number of times to extend the game.

- Feel free to ask the class for their own version of the game!

Stacking wellbeing sessions

Fun activities are a great way of integrating wellbeing into the daily routines of staff and students, but, of course, the bigger impact will come when you look at your whole school's approach.

What I mean by 'whole school approach' in the context of allocating time and routines is making the most of the time when the whole school comes together.

One of the easiest and most effective ways to do this is to look at the concept of 'habit stacking'. Author of *Atomic Habits*, James Clear explains stacking as one of the best ways to build a new habit. You identify a current habit that you already do each day and then 'stack' your new behaviour on top.

This concept is a simple, yet highly effective, way to manufacture wellbeing time across the whole school without causing disruption or adding more unnecessary time.

Let's look at ways you can 'stack' onto what you already have in place. For example, you most likely have regular assemblies, so why not stack a 5–10-minute wellbeing segment into the assembly in one of the following ways.

Principal's message

The principal or a school leader could share a message to reinforce the school values or wellbeing focus. For example, Ben Catalano, Principal of Tenison Woods College in Adelaide, shares a wellbeing message at every assembly. Ben explains:

It's usually picking up on whatever is happening in the school at the time. As a Catholic school, if there is something about helping others, then we focus on feeling good by doing good. If it's celebrating something in or out of school, then it's about character strengths and flourishing.

The principal's message at a whole-school gathering such as an assembly is a fantastic way to address the whole-school wellbeing focus and to acknowledge the 'good' in what is happening as well as addressing what can be improved. This is an easy, yet important, way to keep your program consistent.

Student leader's message

In addition to the principal's message, student leaders can introduce new wellbeing initiatives. For example, at St Peter's College, a boys' school in Adelaide, student leaders deliver a whole range of messages. Deputy Head of the Junior School and wellbeing leader Ben Storer says:

> Our leaders deliver messages on our school values of truth, respect and service. They also start their assemblies with an Acknowledgement of Country in Kaurna language [the original language of Adelaide, South Australia]. The service messaging has been very strong with sharing various ways to connect with community and also having a global mindset.
>
> An example from last year was the 'Light up Vanuatu' project, where the leaders promoted the fundraising campaign. The 'Light up Vanuatu' project is a campaign created by School Aid. The campaign aims to end energy poverty for all the 47 000 children living without energy in Vanuatu. Money raised buys solar lights and their research shows that children with a solar light study 78 per cent longer.

Students presenting wellbeing messages to fellow students is a powerful way to deliver wellbeing as well as providing a sense of ownership.

Wellbeing awards

Wellbeing awards can recognise students who demonstrate skills such as kindness, empathy, gratitude, and so on. For example, at the beginning of her four-year state term, local MP Paula Luethen asked all the school principals in the King electorate in South Australia if they would support an award recognising the kindest student at each year level.

Paula says:

I suggested it could recognise the students who help others, who stand up for others, who say kind things and carry out random acts of kindness. About half my schools introduced the award yearly, and two schools every term. One school, Golden Grove Primary, introduced it for every year level and every term.

Paula is invited along to the schools to present the awards to the recipients, who are selected by the class teacher. Paula continues:

At assemblies and award ceremonies the King Kindness Award [named after Paula's electorate] is announced and often the principal or school leader talks about the value of being kind before the award winners are announced. I present a certificate and say thank you for being the kindest student in your year level.

You could approach your local member of parliament or someone else well respected for support with your awards. It's such a powerful way to promote and recognise students who best demonstrate your school values.

Event and celebration days

When the whole school is together it's an ideal time to promote any wellbeing events and upcoming celebration days.

For example, at Gilles Street Primary School in Adelaide, senior student leaders are given responsibility to announce the wellbeing events and celebration days. Student Wellbeing Leader Meagan Hart shares:

Whether it's Harmony Day, World Gratitude Day or Kindness Day, we hand over the responsibilities to our student leaders. They play a key role in the organisation of the events and also are in charge of the promotion. We find that assemblies are the best place to promote these. Students will provide information, such as dates, the key ideas, show a video promotion or a poster.

Though assemblies were limited during the pandemic, Meagan explains, 'We've adapted by sharing such events via email to staff and families'.

This is a superb way to build excitement around the school leading up to the event. Plus, wellbeing gets recognised and reinforced with all staff, students and, possibly, parents, which is important practice for your whole-school approach. It makes wellbeing visible in front of the whole school.

I'd like for you to now pause and reflect on what you currently do in your school and where you could make time for wellbeing.

OVER TO YOU
Establishing wellbeing routines

Think about what you currently do in your classroom and across the whole school on a consistent basis.

For example, what's your morning routine like?

What do you do as a whole school together?

Make a list of daily, weekly, monthly, term and annual routines or events where you could stack wellbeing on (see the figure 3.2 to help guide you).

I'd encourage you to not be closed minded; be open and list all the ways you think you could stack wellbeing onto what you are already doing. You will most likely be able to fill in more daily and weekly routines

From your list, select one to two ideas that you could start immediately. Then, over the coming weeks, gradually add more to your list.

Daily routines	**Example:** Morning routine: first 10 minutes of the day
Weekly routines	**Example:** Assembly: 10-minute segment
Monthly routines	**Example:** Buddy class: the older year level teaches the younger year level a wellbeing game or activity
Term routines	**Example:** Kindness Award: announcement of the Kindness Awards at assembly
Annual routines	**Example:** Sports Day: recognise the team that demonstrates your school values best on the day

Figure 3.2: Wellbeing routine worksheet

It's time to practise

What you've hopefully seen is that with a few little tweaks to an ordinarily packed schedule, it's easier to make consistent time for wellbeing.

Remember, just like learning and practising skills such as maths, reading or writing, skills such as gratitude, empathy, kindness, positive reflection and service can be, and need to be, practised. We'll look at why you need a variety of these skills next.

As we know, the more we practise, the better we become at the skill—so let's make time to practise!

NOW FOR ACTION
Top tips to try now

1. Identify a space for wellbeing.

   Think about what you already have in place in the classroom and across your school. How can you add on wellbeing to what already exists? For example, adding a 10-minute wellbeing segment into your weekly assembly. Consider including short activities into routines, whether that's a routine for early finishers or morning or afternoon routines. Fill out the table on p.43 to help you with this.

2. Allocate wellbeing time, together.

   Ideally, as a whole school (all classes), allocate wellbeing time into the timetable. Whether that's the first 15 to 30 minutes of each day, one hour a week, creating an extra lesson to include wellbeing or a Wellbeing Wednesday, where the only learning for the day is wellbeing. Time allocation matters—it's that important.

3. Add an Acknowledgement of Country.

In Reconciliation Australia's words:

> *An Acknowledgement of Country is an opportunity for anyone to show respect for Traditional Owners and the continuing connection of Aboriginal and Torres Strait Islander peoples to Country. An Acknowledgement of Country can be offered by any person and like a Welcome to Country, is given at the beginning of a meeting, speech or event.*

If you're not currently doing this, then why not? I recently interviewed Colette Bos, Assistant Principal at Roma Mitchell Secondary College, on my podcast. At the very start, Colette read a beautiful mindfulness and gratitude version (which you can download and use from the Resource Pack) of an Acknowledgement of Country. She explains:

> *This version brings in the contextual approach to wellbeing. It's super important we teach our young people to acknowledge the land we are meeting upon. It's imperative we allow our students to sit and be grateful and reflect on what our traditional owners of our land have done. This type of Acknowledgement of Country is super purposeful.*

This is a simple and very powerful act of gratitude. I encourage you to give it a try.

CHAPTER 4
Address the 5 Habits of Happiness

It was a crisp winter's morning during the school holidays. I was working as a teacher at the time and it was always great to have a couple of weeks away from the school gym to refresh and reset. I was sipping on a cup of instant coffee (please don't hold that against me) and investigating my new-found interest in property investing. Enthusiastic and excited, I had recently discovered that the deposit required to purchase an investment property was nowhere near as much as I had thought.

Motivated to learn more, I was on my laptop googling successful property investors. What happened next was totally unexpected—yet life defining. While I was reading profiles about the big moguls, a pattern started to emerge and it wasn't directly related to property investing at all. I can't remember who the property investors were, but individually they consistently referred to this idea of happiness leading to their success, and, furthermore, gratitude leading to their happiness.

I was instantly intrigued. I didn't yet understand the connection between happiness leading to success and gratitude leading to happiness (let alone its connection to me being able to afford a house!). Soon, the googling switched to 'gratitude leading to happiness'.

What popped up on the results page was my first introduction to positive psychology and positive education: how we help others lead healthy, happy lives.

Traditionally, psychology has been associated with 'waiting' for issues to arise and then helping the person work through the situation. I soon learned that positive psychology was different: it was all about living a good life and thriving. I noticed it was more of an intervention, where we can practise to be happy and practise skills that help us move forward from challenges and make us happier in the present moment. How amazing to teach young students this!

Two clear thoughts stuck in my mind:

- *I wish I had learned this when I was young/at school.*

- *Hang on ... I thought we either bounce back from challenges or we don't, but I didn't know you can actually practise skills like being grateful that will lead you on the path to being more resilient—wow!*

This profound moment was like a shot of adrenaline mixed with a sense of disappointment that I'd only just learned this at the age of about 30.

I felt I had struck gold and if the floss dance had been around at the time, there's a fair chance I would have broken out into an uncoordinated attempt. I always knew the definition of gratitude, for example, but I'd never considered it was something that could be *cultivated* for good health and prosperity.

So I'd love to be able to tell you that from that day on, I practised gratitude every day and that's what led to my ultimate property investing success. In truth, though, the property I purchased soon after was a total lemon. (I still have it today and even in a good market it hasn't gone up a cent.)

The good news is that I've been way more successful with practising gratitude and the other skills that underpin resilience than I was buying that lemon, and as a result, I feel much happier and able to weather life's ebbs and flows, which include being able to deal with the ups and downs of being a property investor.

More importantly, this discovery led me to realise why it is so important that we teach these skills to our kids in school.

Happier for it

Making the discovery that happiness is underpinned by practising certain skills was a complete game changer in my life.

Research by gratitude expert Robert Emmons, in a study of more than 1000 people aged eight to 80, tells us that the consistent practice of gratitude has many physical, psychological and social benefits, including:

- a stronger immune system
- a higher likelihood of exercising more and taking better care of our health
- more optimism and happiness
- being more forgiving
- being more generous, helpful and compassionate.

I've certainly felt some of these effects. How about you?

So imagine if we were to transfer these benefits to our kids. How much healthier would they be? And how much more able would they be to deal with whatever life throws at them (a pandemic and home schooling, for example).

We don't want to wait for mental wellbeing issues to surface; it's about getting on the front foot and helping shape the minds of young people so they are equipped with the skills to deal with challenges because, whether we like it or not, challenges will continue to come. Resilience isn't necessarily a standalone skill; it's the result of practising a combination of skills that lead us to be more resilient and happy.

Resilience isn't necessarily a stand-alone skill; it's the result of practising a combination of skills that lead us to be more resilient and happy.

In addition to gratitude, there are other skills—such as kindness, empathy, positive reflection and serving others—that we can practise to be more resilient and happier.

This realisation is what led to what I now call The 5 Habits of Happiness.

Five habits (not one)

It's really important to practise a *variety* of positive wellbeing habits—not only one.

Stagnation can be an issue when we're learning skills—whether that be playing basketball, practising surfing, playing an instrument or learning a new language. This can come from repeating the same or a similar practice method over and over again. And it's exactly the same with wellbeing programs.

The skills within the program you are aiming to develop across your school, in your classrooms and at home can become stagnant if they don't feature variety.

Yes, gratitude is arguably the most important skill we can master, but the gratitude practice can become boring, especially for kids, even if we're mixing up the practice by having explicit teaching lessons and a variety of activities and games.

So, in terms of helping young people grow their resilience muscle, the great news is, there are other skills we can learn too.

The 5 Habits of Happiness framework (as illustrated in figure 4.1, overleaf) we use at Growing with Gratitude is:

1. *Gratitude*: appreciating the opportunities, the people in your life, the experiences and the things you may take for granted

2. *Empathy*: seeing through another's eyes and understanding how someone is feeling

3. *Kindness*: practising through what you say and what you do

4. *Positive reflection*: focusing on the good things and understanding that what has happened, has happened, and that it's what you do next that's important

5. *Service*: serving others without expecting anything in return.

Let's take a closer look at each habit now, starting with Gratitude.

Habit 1: Gratitude

Dear Mum and Dad

Thank you for taking me to my wonderful school and letting me have a good education. Thank you, Dad, for being my school basketball coach and taking your time off work to come and help my friends and I get better. Thank you, Mum, for being my mum and taking me to wonderful places when Dad is not there. I thank you so much that I am alive. Thank you so much for being you.

From me, your thankful girl.

I love you.

Every time I work with a group of students, no matter their age, I always look to include an activity where we practise reflecting on the people or things in our life that we may take for granted. Providing the opportunity for students to write an appreciation

5 Habits of Happiness

The great news is, just like learning a skill in a sport, the 5 Habits of Happiness can be practised.

Gratitude

appreciating the opportunities, the people in your life, the experiences and the things you may take for granted.

Empathy

Seeing through another's eyes and understanding how someone is feeling.

Kindness

Practising through what you say and what you do.

Positive Reflection

Focusing on the good things and understanding that what has happened, has happened, and that it's what you do next that's important.

Service

Serving others without expecting anything in return.

Figure 4.1: The 5 Habits of Happiness

letter—like the one Abigail from Highgate School wrote—to people in their life who do wonderful things for them, is a great way to practise appreciation.

Now, we all may have our subtleties on what gratitude means. But I like the following definition by Sansone and Sansone: 'the appreciation of what is valuable and meaningful to oneself and represents a general state of thankfulness and/or appreciation'.

And I couldn't agree more with Emmons and Mishra, who suggest, 'that gratitude, as a virtue, is deliberately cultivated. It needs to be taught, modelled, practiced until it becomes a habit'.

Leading with gratitude is a great place to start and, if it so happens that you can only practise one of the five habits, I'd highly recommend gratitude. Research tells us there are numerous social, psychological, physical-health and personality benefits that come from a consistent practise of gratitude.

These include (but are not limited to):

- being more optimistic
- making us more giving
- greater access to social support
- better relationships
- making more people like us
- increasing self-esteem
- keeping suicidal thoughts at bay
- making us happier
- being more likely to exercise
- improving sleep
- reducing depressive symptoms
- lowering blood pressure.

Indeed, gratitude is powerful. It can also help us reframe challenges, no matter how big or small, to see them from a more positive point of view: coming from a place of being grateful.

So, as teachers, parents and educators, we want to look at ways of developing this critical skill—and that starts at home and in the classroom.

Here's an activity you might like to try.

OVER TO YOU
Four corners

A great gratitude activity relates to reflecting on four areas of life. It's fantastic for the classroom, in staff meetings and for home.

How it works:

- Provide a piece of paper for each student or download The 4 Corners of Gratitude template from the Resource Pack (see figure 4.2).

- If you are using a blank piece of paper, have students write the following in the corners of the page:

    1. *People*: the people in my life I am grateful for and why (top left)

    2. *Opportunities*: the opportunities I am grateful for (top right)

    3. *Experiences*: the experiences I am grateful for (bottom left)

    4. *Take for granted*: the things I sometimes take for granted (bottom right).

- Once students are ready, have them respond to each question by writing their answers under the relevant heading. You could instruct students to choose one response per question, or a few.

- As a debrief, discuss their answers in a group. Sometimes we can forget to stop and reflect on the things we should be grateful for and this concept is a simple way to remind us to reflect, focusing on the four areas.

The 4 Corners of Gratitude

People
The people in my life I am grateful for and why.

_____

_____

_____

_____

Opportunities
The opportunities I am grateful for.

_____

_____

_____

_____

Experiences
The experiences I am grateful for.

_____

_____

_____

Take for granted
The things I sometimes take for granted.

_____

_____

_____

GROWING WITH GRATITUDE

Figure 4.2: Four Corners of Gratitude

Habit 2: Empathy

I love this quote by Alfred Alder: 'Empathy is seeing with the eyes of another, listening with the ears of another, and feeling with the heart of another'.

When you discuss empathy with students, they often identify it as treating others how you want to be treated (the golden rule), walking in other people's shoes or understanding how someone is feeling. These are all good places to start.

The tricky thing is that empathy can be challenging to learn (even for adults), particularly for young people who are at the stage in life where they are developing the awareness to understand *how* others view the world and are also developing the ability to understand other people's emotions, as well as their own.

Let me tell you a story to illustrate my point.

During a Saturday morning under-9s school soccer match, you could see the frustration building up in one of our players from a mile away. We will call him James. James is one of the better players in the team and it just wasn't his day. The opposition was strong, our team was missing passes, our dribbling skills were off and at the same time the other team was very cohesive.

I was watching James and you could see the frustration kick in. He was very animated in his gestures towards teammates and he began to be extra aggressive with multiple rough slide tackles on opposition. The referee was rightly awarding free kicks against James and this added to his frustration. And the parent yelling at the ref didn't help one bit.

James crossed the line a couple of minutes later, when again the ref awarded a justified free kick against him. This set James off. The 16-year-old referee copped it and James's extreme levels of negative emotions overwhelmed him, which resulted in tears flowing.

I wasn't coaching the team, but I was watching, representing the school as the co-ordinator. The coach did the right thing and brought James off for a chance to calm down.

I gave James a few minutes to himself and then I took him aside.

James, how you feeling? I could see you were getting quite frustrated out there. I understand why: sport can be very emotional and frustrating at times. Now that you've calmed down, do you think arguing with the referee in the way you did was the right thing to do?

He shook his head.

I asked James, who was still teary eyed, 'If you were refereeing and a player went off at you, how would you feel?'

James responded, 'I wouldn't like it.'

'And what if we didn't have referees. Would we be able to play the game?'

The next week I had James for a PE lesson. We played a game of indoor hockey and for part of it, I got James to umpire.

Afterwards I asked him, 'James, how did you find umpiring?'

James responded by saying, 'It was okay; a lot harder than I thought'.

This was a perfect way to hammer home the point. Once we get the feel for how hard refereeing can be, we start to see things from another's perspective. There were no further issues with James's on-field behaviour.

This is a great example of how we can teach and demonstrate empathy to our kids. And it's really important because the negative effects of *not* learning empathy is that we can end up with bullying behaviour issues.

Research from Salavera and colleagues concludes that 'teachers and other members of the school community should work on empathy with young people from an early age, in order to help students and reduce bullying in the classroom'.

I strongly believe that bullying shouldn't exist if our children are being taught empathy skills from a young age.

A simple way to look at it is, 'I don't like to be bullied, so I am not going to bully anyone else'. That's what we're trying to encourage.

Research concludes that the benefits of empathy include:

- improved relationships with others
- better social relationships
- enabling you to be more helpful to others
- boosting self-esteem
- being better able to accept others
- helping to deliver bad news
- being better at collaborating in groups
- greater awareness of self and others
- being able to see situations from other people's point of view.

Empathy is also important for helping us to reframe situations by using our self-talk to see things from another person's or group of people's point of view.

Let's look at a way you can instil empathy in the classroom by playing a game.

OVER TO YOU
Empathy basketball

The purpose of this game is for students to put themselves in another person's situation as a way of finding out how it feels.

This game is played from the point of view of someone with a visual impairment. If you don't have access to a basketball hoop, then a bin, a box or a washing basket will work fine. You could use a soft, squishy ball or even a bundled pair of socks.

How to play:

1. In pairs, player 1 is blindfolded and given a ball within shooting distance of the hoop. Player 2 is the guide.

2. The guide instructs the shooter by using verbal instructions (no physical directing) to position the shooter and give them the cues of where to aim, and so on.

3. Once in position, the shooter shoots the ball. If unsuccessful, the guide will give feedback for turn 2. After five or six shots, players swap roles.

The guide's role is also to protect all blindfolded players when the ball bounces off the ring.

Be sure to highlight the purpose of the game and ask the students to 'really observe how you feel not being able to see'.

It's really important to debrief this activity. Ask the players to describe how they felt not being able to see while they were shooting. They'll say things like:

- I wasn't too sure of what was around me

- With the noise I found it hard to hear

- I felt I had to rely on someone else

- I was worried I was going to bump into something or someone else.

(continued)

A great follow-up question is, 'What could come up at school —
whether that be in the classroom or out in the yard — where you
could put yourself in other people's shoes?'

They might say:

- If I see someone on their own, I'll invite them to
  play/ask them to join in.
- If I see someone hurt, I will help them.

You could also ask questions to drive the conversation:

- What if a new student started at the school — what
  could you do?
- What if you saw someone hurt — what could you do?
- What if someone was sitting on their own — what could you do?
- If you saw someone hurt, why would you help them? Why
  wouldn't you just leave them there?

Encourage players to put themselves in other people's shoes as
often as they can. You'll be amazed by what they share!

Habit 3: Positive reflection

After learning about positive reflection in class, year-7 student
Hannah wanted to practise it at home with her family.

Hannah, her brother, her mum and her dad took it in turns
to reflect on a highlight of their day. Hannah, her mum and her
brother shared their highlights. Then it was her dad's turn.

Interestingly, Dad responded by saying, 'I can tell you what
wasn't great about my day'.

Reflecting on this story was a reminder that there's a good
chance Hannah's dad had grown up focusing on the negatives,

rather than being given the opportunity to train his brain to think about the positives. How many of us can relate to that?

This isn't necessarily his fault; it's probably the way he's been conditioned since he was young.

As humans, our brains are wired to focus on the negatives. This is known as the negativity bias. I like this summary from the Decision Lab: 'Negativity bias occurs even when adverse events and positive events are of the same magnitude, meaning we feel negative events more intensely'.

Psychologist Catherine Moore shares some examples. We often:

- recall and think about insults more than compliments
- respond more — emotionally and physically — to aversive stimuli
- dwell on unpleasant or traumatic events more than pleasant ones
- focus our attention more quickly on negative rather than positive information.

Think of a day recently, where a number of good things happened and perhaps one not so good. If you are like the majority of us, it's likely you focused on the not-so-good for way longer than the positives. However, research suggests we can train our brain to focus on the 'good things' — *but* it takes practice.

This is why it's really important to practise positive reflection.

Positive reflection is similar to having a growth mindset. It's about focusing on the good things, rather than the negative. It's also about understanding, in challenging situations, that what has happened, has happened, and that it's what you do next that's important. It's also about reflecting on how you can get better, even if you are already good at something.

With positive reflection, you can:

- improve self-esteem
- become better at wanting to improve
- see challenges as opportunities
- lower rates of depression
- lower levels of distress and pain
- have greater resistance to illnesses
- have better psychological and physical wellbeing
- have better coping skills during hardships and times of stress
- have an increased life span
- be better able to use self-talk to put situations in perspective
- be better at setting goals
- be better at recovering from challenges.

So, what are some ways you can encourage this in your school and at home?

OVER TO YOU
End-of-week reflections

On a Friday, have your students reflect on their week (you can also do this with your children at home). Ideally, each student should have a Positive Reflection exercise book for the activity.

For younger students, and as an alternative if you are out of time, make it verbal by students sharing in small groups or pairs (as we all know, it can take them half a day to get a book and a pencil out).

Ask students to spend one minute writing about the best part of their day.

1. Write three things you did for someone else. For example:

    - On Monday, I showed Kelly around our school. She's new, so I offered to show her around.

    - On Wednesday after school, I helped an elderly person by carrying their shopping to their car because the bags were heavy for them to carry.

    - On Thursday, I invited Rodney to join in our game of handball because he was sitting on his own.

2. Write three things you did to improve yourself. For example:

    - I read 10 pages of a book about being a good friend.

    - I went for a run with Dad.

    - I went out in the backyard and practised my basketball shooting.

3. Identify one thing you are looking forward to over the weekend and say why. For example:

    - I am looking forward to going to Nadia's birthday party. I am looking forward to it because all my friends will be there and she's going to have the best birthday cake ever.

4. Choose your own reflection question. For example:

    - What was something you learned this week?

    - What do you want to get better at, even though you are already good at it?

    - What's a goal you want to achieve next week?

In a perfect world, students will reflect on all of these. If time is an issue, choose one or two of the reflections or have students share verbally.

You could also choose to ask one or two of the reflection questions at the end of every day.

Habit 4: Kindness

I was kind to my gymnastics coach, Brenton. He felt surprised because we normally don't listen that much. It made me feel grateful because he saw me do that. Also, today I felt that I have to do something for someone that I haven't done before.

Penny

I carried out my random act of kindness at school and it was for Mr Humphrys. I told him, 'thanks for teaching me'. I think that Mr Humphrys was happy that I appreciated him teaching me. This made me feel happy that Mr Humphrys was happy that I was being nice.

James

Today I complimented Eve on how she looked. When I complimented Eve she looked at me with a confusing look and asked what I had said. I said it again and she replied, 'Oh, thanks'. Doing this random act of kindness made me feel really happy, as if I was a part of trying to make a happier nation. I am also proud of myself for doing this and am excited for tomorrow night's dishwasher kindness act.

Jenny

My act of kindness was to do Adelaide's hair for school. I did this at home. I did this because it meant my mum could help Freddie. My sister felt happy (her words). I felt like I was helping my mum because Freddie was sick and she had to be with him twenty-four seven.

Arlo

These are four examples of kindness reflections that Brett Humphrys's year-5 class came up with while he was teaching at Immanuel Primary. Over a five-week period, Brett asked his class to reflect on acts of kindness they had completed that day or the day before. Such reflection allows students to contemplate the impact they may have had on others through their kindness. Brett also reported that parents had noticed changes in students' behaviour over this period.

We often hear about 'random acts of kindness', but we like to encourage 'planned acts of kindness', such as the ones the kids came up with above.

Planned acts of kindness are a great way for young people to start practising kindness. By planning, we are setting up opportunities for young people to practise being kind. This is an important stepping stone in making kindness a habit.

These planned acts help to:

- release feel-good chemicals in our brain
- create a sense of belonging and reduce isolation
- keep things in perspective
- make the world a happier place—one act of kindness can often lead to more!
- make others happy and make you happy
- reduce anxiety and stress levels
- make other people's lives a little easier or better.

It is tremendous that we have a World Kindness Day, but it's not enough—we need to practise kindness every day. Here are some examples of how to help do this.

OVER TO YOU
The 7-Day Kindness Challenge

This challenge involves students planning seven days of acts of kindness and then carrying them out at a designated time.

Discuss with students examples of acts of kindness first. These acts of kindness do not have to be big things. For example:

- holding the door open for someone

- picking up litter without being asked

- asking someone to join a game

- taking out the rubbish.

Also, highlight that doing acts of kindness is about doing it and not expecting anything in return.

On the 7-Day Kindness Challenge planner (see figure 4.3), students plan out their seven days of kindness. (You'll find the planner in the Resource Pack.)

After the kindness act, ask your students to reflect on how it made them feel doing the act of kindness. If they did an act of kindness for someone, how did the person receiving it feel?

7-Day Kindness Challenge

	Act of kindness	How I felt ...	How did the person feel?
DAY 1			
DAY 2			
DAY 3			
DAY 4			
DAY 5			
DAY 6			
DAY 7			

GROWING WITH GRATITUDE

Figure 4.3: The 7-Day Kindness Challenge planner

Habit 5: Service

A dad walked in to teacher Tiff's year-3 classroom: 'What have you done to my son?' he asked.

Stunned, Tiff responded with, 'Ahhh, what do you mean?'

'He's doing things around our house to help out without being asked. He's never done this before. What did you do?'

Relieved, Tiff explained: 'We've been practising service. We've been learning about how it's important to do things for others without expecting anything in return. We also discussed that the home is a great place to start serving and being helpful. As the dad walked out of the classroom he said, 'Well, thank you. Please keep practising'.

This is a real story from a school that shows how wonderful the 5 Habits of Happiness can be when practised both at school and at home. Service really does start in the home (something one of my principals often reminded everyone at assembly). Home is a perfect place for young people to start serving, followed by school and then in the community.

These skills are easily transferrable to all contexts, which is why I want to encourage them.

When we 'serve', we look outside of ourselves, beyond our own problems, and seek to bring value to others without expecting anything in return.

This will help us to:

- be happier
- put things in perspective
- have a sense of purpose
- build a sense of belonging
- feel connected to others
- increase our self-esteem

- reduce depression

- contribute to something far bigger than ourselves.

Let's look at some activities that encourage students to serve at home.

OVER TO YOU
Operation Home Service

This home service activity can be planned in the classroom and then carried out at home (or just completed at home).

But note, the home service students are planning should be in addition to any usual chores they are required to carry out and should not be rewarded with pocket money. The activity is about serving without expecting anything in return.

Get students to plan out seven days of home service.

Table 4.1 is an example of home service tasks that could be planned.

Table 4.1: Home service planner example

Day	Task	Family member signature
Monday	Take out the bins	
Tuesday	Clean my and my sister's room	
Wednesday	Load the dishwasher	
Thursday	Clean the dog kennel	
Friday	Vacuum the house	
Saturday	Clear the table for everyone after breakfast	
Sunday	Help set up for dinner	

Once the planner is complete, stick it on the fridge and have students work through their home service tasks. Then have a family member sign off. You can find the planner in the Resource Pack.

Why we practise the 5 habits

So now you've got a variety of skills and strategies up your sleeve you can start to play with.

But before we move on, it's important to remember one thing.

Something I've noticed over my wellbeing journey is that we rarely explain to our kids *why* we are doing these things. For example, why practise gratitude? Yes, research tells us gratitude helps us move forward from challenges and trauma—but how? How do we use gratitude to benefit us?

It's really important we work at ways of communicating why we are doing something to our kids because this is what will help make the habits stick.

This involves understanding how our self-talk impacts us.

By practising gratitude on a consistent basis, over time our kids will likely become proficient at putting things in perspective by reframing and emotionally regulating themselves. This involves using self-talk and coming from a place of gratitude. For example, *What Ruby said to me before made me quite upset, but to be honest, when it comes down to it, is it really that bad? I do have lots of great friends who I am grateful for. Maybe Ruby was just having a bad day. I'm also lucky I go to a great school and I also know how lucky I am to have a home to go home to later, so looking at it that way it's not really so bad.*

It's unlikely the change will happen overnight, but explaining and modelling how students can use self-talk, coming from the angle of being grateful, is one of the most powerful skills we can possess.

Here's an example of how I reframe, coming from a place of being grateful from a teaching perspective: *Today has been a tough day; the parent confrontation at the end of the day was the worst way to finish, as it had already been a stressful day with assessment and the students just seemed to be off. But you know what, if I actually stop and think about it, maybe it's not so bad. I am grateful I have a home to go to, where I can relax, and I am grateful I have a job at this amazing school. This day was just one of those days.*

Reframing is a strategy I've used for a decade and it's been life changing. It's helped me put things in perspective and has been instrumental in helping me move forward from all kinds of challenges.

It's really important to share with students that there's nothing wrong with negative emotions such as feeling sad, mad, angry, frustrated or annoyed. It's going to happen: we're human and it's totally okay to feel these emotions. However, it's good to know what to do if you're having a bad day or going through a rough time and reframing is a strategy that could help.

When I go into a school and explain reframing, I never say, 'You have to try this'. The language is around, 'Here's a strategy you can give a go'. It's about planting the seed and introducing a strategy that can help them move forward from the small, day-to-day frustrations or more significant challenges that may come up.

As I noted earlier, another important element is modelling to students and adults: how they can use self-talk to see things from a more positive point of view coming from a place of gratitude. A further key step in the modelling process is asking.

Me: Do you think it's easy to use self-talk like this or do you think it takes practice?

Response: I think it takes practice (the most common response).

Me: And what generally happens the more we practise something?

Response: We get better.

Me: And it's exactly the same with gratitude. The more we practise, the easier it becomes to see things from a more positive point of view, coming from a place of being grateful—but practice is the key.

(In the Resource Pack, you can download a script that will guide you through a conversation like this.)

I have found this to be one of the most forgotten parts of teaching: wellbeing for students. And it's even more powerful when you share your experience with how, for example, you've used gratitude in your life.

Helping them to understand why they are learning what they are and how they can apply it in their own life to help them and others—this is the real power of wellbeing programs.

In the next chapter, we'll take this a step further and look at ways you can make this whole process fun and enjoyable.

NOW FOR ACTION
One-day action challenge

This is a challenge I'd encourage you to do with your students or at home as a family. I'd also highly recommend giving the challenge a go yourself with your students or in your own time. The challenge is to complete all five habits of happiness activities in one day. Each activity won't take too long...so who's in?

1. Do a gratitude activity
    Write what you are grateful for today. Ideas: gratitude jar, journal.

2. Appreciate your friends
    Ask them if they are okay. Write a letter to a friend or family member expressing why you appreciate them.

3. Reflect on the great things
    Spend two minutes writing down the best part of your day and two ways you helped someone else today.

4. Practise empathy
    We don't know what other people are going through. Reach out to a friend or family member and offer them a hand.

5. Do something kind/serve others
    What can I do to be helpful? What act of kindness can I do for someone today?

CHAPTER 5
Make it fun

In August of 2014, I had the wonderful opportunity to work with Dr Deborah Green and Dr Deborah Price (who wrote the foreword for this book) of the University of South Australia. Deborah Price is currently Research Degree Coordinator and Senior Lecturer in Inclusive Education and Wellbeing (as well as wearing many other hats). She's led a number of significant projects and, since 2017, has been president of the Australian Curriculum Studies Association (ACSA).

We conducted a small research project with a group of students at Immanuel Primary School, where I was teaching at the time, in Adelaide. The project involved year 1–6 students. For six weeks they were required to participate in some daily and weekly activities at home. The daily activities included writing down three things they were grateful for and spending two minutes writing about the best part of their day. The weekly activities included doing a planned act of kindness and something around home in the way of service (in addition to the usual chores and not receiving any extra pocket money).

At the end of the six weeks each student completed a survey and was interviewed. One of the questions the students responded to was, 'Were there any activities you didn't like?'

What was very interesting and turned out to be extremely profound was that 100 per cent of the students reported they didn't like writing three things they were grateful for each day. One student reported, 'I just found it a bit hard to come up with new suggestions for three things I am grateful for every day'. Another reflected by saying; 'It was a bit much to write three things I was grateful for each day'.

Surprised to hear this? I was.

This was an extremely significant discovery because at the time (and still now) this kind of journaling was 'the in thing'. Research was telling us that a great way to practise being happier is to practise gratitude by writing down three things we are grateful for each day.

Now, don't get me wrong. I still think journaling is a great way to start practising gratitude, but on an ongoing basis, it can be repetitive and become a chore—especially for young minds.

It didn't necessarily mean the students weren't grateful; it simply meant this way of practising gratitude perhaps wasn't the best method for this kind of group. It seemed quite the chore and boring for these youngsters and, therefore, wasn't having the desired impact.

Our learnings led us to this conclusion:

To keep our kids engaged with gratitude and wellbeing, we need to make it fun!

Variety is the spice of life

I put my PE teacher hat on and pondered: *In PE lessons, what are the students doing when they are most engaged and having the most fun?* And straight away playing games came to mind.

A mix of games, ongoing projects, lessons and activities is a perfect formula for teaching gratitude and other positive skills to students. In his book *All Work No Play*, my great mate and colleague Dale Sidebottom explains the benefit of playing games and keeping learning fun as a fantastic way to engage students. Dale writes:

> *When play is used to teach, the environment often becomes positive and enthusiastic almost instantly—it's magical. So, I always encourage teachers to teach through play if appropriate and possible, and kids to learn through play, particularly if they find sitting still while listening and reading difficult.*

Research from Plass and colleagues also shows that using games in teaching can help increase student participation, foster social and emotional learning, and motivate students to take risks.

Have a think about for how long and how often you fill out your own gratitude journal. It's easy to fall off the horse, so to speak, when it comes to the practice. Like the students, you may feel it becomes a chore, despite being a good way to start your practice.

In the research project with Dr Deborah Price and Dr Deborah Green, we discovered that variety was really important in keeping students engaged and actively learning.

There's little doubt repetition is a good thing when it comes to learning and maintaining new skills, but we had to address the fact that 100 per cent of the students found writing three things they were grateful for each day for six weeks 'boring'. So, the takeaway was, *We need to provide opportunities for students to practise—in this case gratitude—on a consistent basis, but in a variety of ways to keep it fun, fresh and engaging.*

Fresh long-term perspectives

It's important to remember that the practice of wellbeing is a marathon, not a sprint, so we need to carefully think about how we practise wellbeing for the long term, so that it's fun, engaging and includes variety. The issue is that we have a focus for a while on a topic—for example, gratitude—we pick up an activity or two for a while, but then we abandon it. It's so important to always look at ways to improve and keep things interesting.

American Philosopher John Dewey put it this way: 'You cannot teach today the same way you did yesterday to prepare students for tomorrow'. Words to live by!

So, I want to propose some ideas that could be new for you. In fact, they may open your eyes to brand new ways to teach wellbeing to students in the classroom, as well as initiatives across your whole school. We will also explore how the school and home can work synergistically to enhance wellbeing.

You will be able to implement some of the ideas I'm about to share with you immediately. However, there are others that you'll need to come back to when the time is right.

In chapter 3 I spoke of the importance of routines and ways we can build wellbeing practice into our day, week, term and so on. And it's in these routines that we want to experiment with a variety of activities.

So let's look at some games you can try, and ways you can reward your students for sticking with them.

The game of life

Games are the perfect way to make wellbeing fun and engaging in the classroom. The examples I'm going to share are a mix of gratitude, empathy, positive reflection and self-awareness games (remember, variety is the key). Some are short and some longer. And what's even better, you can download game templates and full instructions for free from the Resource Pack.

'Gratitude Showdown'

The game 'Gratitude Showdown' is an alternative to a simple gratitude reflection.

Here's how it goes:

- At any stage during the school day, call out 'Gratitude Showdown'. Students should organise themselves into pairs or small groups.

- Ask students a specific question, such as 'What do we have in our classroom that you are grateful for?'

- Then say, 'Go!' Students go back and forth for 1 minute reflecting on what they're grateful for.

- One student might say, 'I am grateful for the aircon in the room'; another might say, 'I am grateful for the smart-board we learn from'. Students take it in turns to come up with as many answers as possible.

- You could create a challenge to see who comes up with the most answers over a certain number of minutes.

Of course, you'll need to make sure everyone is clear on how you play the game before you begin. This could be done prior to the first time you play, so that as soon as you say 'Gratitude Showdown' students will know what to do.

'Gratitude Yahtzee'

'Gratitude Yahtzee' is played in a similar way to traditional Yahtzee, but this version includes gratitude, positive reflection and kindness repetitions, as well as physical activity challenges.

It can be played as a fun competitive game or as a fun individual activity (keep in mind, the larger the group, the longer the game will be).

Each player will need:

- a player sheet (you'll find a template in the Resource Pack; see figure 5.1)

- a pencil or pen

- five dice (between the pair/group, or five dice each if playing individually)

- a dice cup (to roll the dice from)

- a clipboard (for something to lean on, if playing on a soft surface such as carpet).

How to play:

Players roll one dice each and the player with the highest number goes first.

1. *First roll:* Roll all five dice. For example, if you roll Yahtzee (all numbers the same), mark your player sheet right away. Otherwise, continue with your second roll.

2. *Second roll:* Set aside any keepers and re-roll the rest. Don't like any of them? Re-roll them all. If you get the exact combo you need, mark your player sheet. Otherwise, continue with your third roll.

3. *Third and final roll:* If you still haven't created a combo, or just want to maximise your score, roll some or all of your dice (as above)—even any keepers you might have set aside. You must enter a score at the end of this roll, whether or not you like your dice. If your roll doesn't suit any of your empty boxes, you have to enter a zero somewhere. *But remember:* scoring even a single dice value is better than a zero.

Gratitude Yahtzee player sheet

SECTION 1	INSTRUCTIONS
Ones (only add up the total number of ones) SCORE _____	Write down someone you are grateful for and say why.
Twos (only add up the total number of twos) SCORE _____	What is an experience you are grateful for? What is something in the room you are grateful for?
Threes (only add up the total number of threes) SCORE _____	Write 3 things you are looking forward to: 1. 2. 3.
Fours (only add up the total number of fours) SCORE _____	Complete 4 burpees
Fives (only add up the total number of fives) SCORE _____	Complete 5 burpees
Sixes (only add up the total number of sixes) SCORE _____	Complete 6 push-ups

TOTAL SCORE

GROWING WITH GRATITUDE

Figure 5.1: Gratitude Yahtzee player sheet (cont'd on page 82)

Gratitude Yahtzee player sheet

SECTION 2	INSTRUCTIONS
3 of a kind (add up the total of all dice) SCORE _____	What has been the best part of your week so far?
4 of a kind (add up the total of all dice) SCORE _____	What is an act of kindness you could do for someone today?
Full House (3 of 1 number and 2 of another = 25 points) SCORE _____	What is something you could do at home today to help out?
Straight (sequence of 4 numbers = 30 points) SCORE _____	Have a stare-off. The first person to laugh runs a lap around the room/gym (10 push-ups if in a smaller area)
Chance (add up the total of all 5 dice) SCORE _____	Choose and complete one of the following: 1. 10 squats 2. Run on the spot for 10 seconds 3. 10 sit-ups
Yahtzee (5 of the same number = 50 points) SCORE _____	If you roll a Yahtzee, everyone in your group completes 20 star jumps. If you don't roll a Yahtzee you complete 20 star jumps.

TOTAL SCORE (both sections)

GROWING WITH GRATITUDE

Figure 5.1: Gratitude Yahtzee player sheet (cont'd)

4. *Activity:* Once a player enters their score for the round, they must immediately complete an activity. Alongside where players enter each score on the player sheet you will find an instruction. Some activities will require a written response (e.g. gratitude activities) and some will be a physical activity (e.g. do five push-ups). The activity must be completed before the next player has their turn.

Players add up their player sheets once they have completed each box. Add up section 1 and section 2 separately and then add up the total score.

'Gratitude Skittles'

'Gratitude Skittles' (the confectionary type) is a fun and engaging way to practise gratitude in the classroom, in a staff meeting or at home.

You will need:

- a fun-size pack of Skittles per player (a set of coloured counters for each player will also work—the colours need to match the five coloured dots on the Gratitude Skittles game sheet: see figure 5.2, overleaf)

- one Gratitude Skittles game sheet per player (you'll find a template in the Resource Pack)

- a pen or pencil for each player.

How to play:

- Print off a Gratitude Skittles game sheet for each player.

- Hand out the fun-size packs of Skittles (or counters) to the players and have them open their packet. Instruct them to leave the skittles in the packet.

- Like a lucky dip, players take one skittle at a time from the pack. For example, if a player picks an orange skittle, they write the answer to the question next to the orange dot on the game sheet.

Gratitude Skittles

RED — Who is a person you are grateful for?

_____

_____

ORANGE — What is a skill you have that you are grateful for?

_____

_____

YELLOW — Name an experience you are grateful for.

_____

_____

GREEN — What is an opportunity you have had that you are grateful for?

_____

_____

PURPLE — What's something you are grateful for about your school?

_____

_____

Figure 5.2: 'Gratitude Skittles'

- Repeat the process until all players have answered all five questions.

- If a player picks a colour skittle that they have already answered the question for, they can eat the skittle and then pick again.

- Once the game is finished, have students share their responses. You could do this by going around the room, asking people to share, or sharing in small groups.

Variations

- Have players create questions, or create your own questions, that match with each skittle colour.

- Play as a group, with groups of students sitting in circles. Print out and place a Gratitude Skittles game sheet in the middle of the group. Instead of writing answers down, players call their response to each question out loud to their group.

Conclude the game by highlighting that gratitude can be practised in many ways, and that it can be fun to practise gratitude. Then ask students, 'What happens the more we practise?'

Go on to explain, 'The more you practise gratitude, the better you will get at it. And you may just start to see things from a more positive point of view, especially if you are having a bad day. But it does take practice'.

It's important to be consistent with gratitude and other positive habit-forming practices such as kindness, empathy, positive reflection and serving others. And, as educators and family members, it's important we provide the opportunity for people to practise.

'Gratitude Cards'

Playing cards is a fantastic way to engage kids in games and learning simultaneously. Cards can be played as a fun competitive game or as an individual activity. Best of all, it's yet another way you can practise gratitude in a game situation.

You will need:

- a pack of playing cards per group/pair/student
- 'Gratitude Cards' game sheets—one per player (you'll find a template in the Resource Pack; see figure 5.3).
- a pencil or pen for each player
- a clipboard (for something to lean on, if playing on a soft surface such as carpet).

How to play:

'Gratitude Cards' can be played in small groups, in pairs or individually (keep in mind, the larger the group, the longer the game will be). I recommend groups of three to five.

To see who goes first, each player picks a card randomly from the pack. The player with the highest card goes first (place those cards back into the pack).

1. Each player has a game sheet and pen/pencil in front of them, ready to play. Groups of students sit in circles.

2. The cards are placed face down, mixed up, in the middle of the group.

3. Player 1 randomly picks a card from the mixed-up pile and flips the card. For example, if the card is a 4 of any suit, the player looks at the game sheet, reads the instruction beside the number 4 and completes the activity. *Note:* it doesn't matter what suit is picked up; it's the number that counts.

Gratitude Cards

Ace
Place a sticky note on something in the room that you are grateful for.

Two
Name two people in your life that you are grateful for and say why.

Three
Name three things that make you happy.

Four
What is something that made you laugh recently?

Five
What are five ways to be kind to someone?
Hint: it could be through what you say or something you do.

Six
You have 6 seconds to make your partner or someone in your group laugh.

Seven
What have you got coming up in your life that you are really looking forward to? And how does it make you feel when you think about it?

Eight
Complete 8 sit-ups.

Nine
Complete 9 push-ups.

Ten
Gratitude challenge
Set a timer for 30 seconds and see if you can name 10 things you are grateful for (people, opportunities, experiences or things).

Jack
Complete 10 jumping jacks (star jumps).

Queen
Who is a person you admire and why?

King
What has someone done for you recently? Your challenge is to thank them by either saying thank you or writing a thank you note.

GROWING WITH GRATITUDE

Figure 5.3: 'Gratitude Cards' game sheet

4. Once player 1 has completed their short activity, it's player 2's turn to pick up a card and do their activity (move clockwise around the group), then player 3's turn, and so on.

5. If a player picks up a card and they've already completed that activity, the card goes straight to the used pile and it's the next player's turn.

6. The game continues until a player has filled up their game sheet.

'Rapid Fire'

The purpose of this game is to practise self-awareness via a fun and fast-paced game. With very little time to think, players are challenged to respond to statements/questions.

This is a fantastic way to get in touch with your thoughts and feelings, as well as to get to know other people.

The game is best played in pairs (you can have players switch partners during the game).

How to play:

- Open the 'Rapid Fire—Self-Awareness Game' Power-Point (you can download this for free from the Resource Pack) and display it on a screen so all players can see. See figure 5.4.

- PowerPoint slides 2 to 17 each feature a statement or a question participants need to respond to, as well as a 30-second countdown clock (press 'enter' or 'next' on your clicker to start the 30-second countdown timer).

- As soon as the countdown timer begins, player 1 has 15 seconds to respond to the statement or question. Once 15 seconds is up, player 2 responds to the same statement/question (note: the timer will continue for 30 seconds without stopping).

- Once the first slide is complete, immediately click through to the next slide and repeat. The 30-second countdown timer will automatically start again when you press 'enter' or 'next' on your clicker.

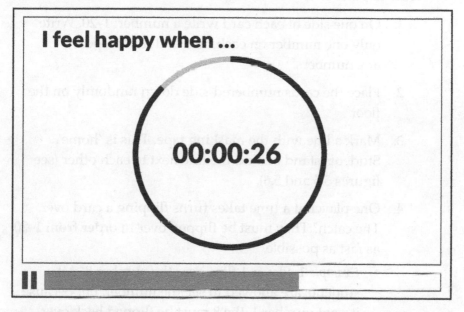

I feel happy when ...

00:00:26

Figure 5.4: 'Rapid Fire'

'Flipper'

The purpose of 'Flipper' is for players to work together to achieve a goal, demonstrate self-control/emotional regulation skills in a frustrating situation and understand they can work through challenging situations to achieve goals. The game is super fun and engaging.

You will need:

- masking tape (or markers)
- A5 cards labelled 1–20 (one set for each group).

Goal:

- In teams of 3–4, players work together to flip over the cards labelled 1–20 in the correct order as quickly as possible.

How to play:

1. On one side of each card write a number: 1–20. Write only one number on each card and don't repeat any numbers.

2. Place the cards numbered-side down randomly on the floor.

3. Mark a line with the masking tape. This is 'home'. Students stand behind the line next to each other (see figures 5.5 and 5.6).

4. One player at a time takes turns flipping a card over. The catch? They must be flipped over in order from 1–20 as fast as possible.

   - *Example 1.* Player 1 flips over the number 8. All students are allowed to see the number, but because it's not number 1, the 8 must be flipped back over, face down. The idea is players observe where the 8 was, so when it comes to finding number 8, they have an idea where it is.

   - *Example 2.* Player 1 flips over the number 1. Great: that's the first number in the sequence. It stays facing up. Player 1 has another turn and aims to flip number 2. If the next number is not 2, they flip the card back over and the next person has a turn.

Rules:

1. One student at a time crosses the line to take a turn.

2. If the number on the card they flip over is not the next one in the sequence, the card must be flipped back over in the same place to hide the number.

Figure 5.5: Students playing 'Flipper'

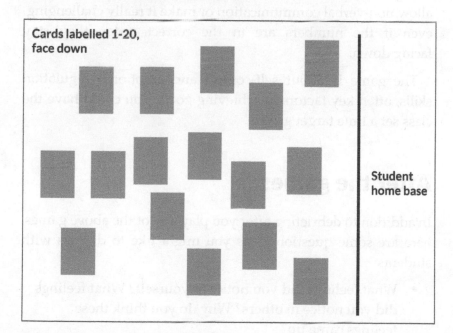

Cards labelled 1-20,
face down

Student
home base

Figure 5.6: 'Flipper' game set-up

3. If the number on the card is in the correct order, the student flips another card. If the next card is not the next consecutive number, the student returns back to home base.

4. Ensure each student has a turn before starting second turns.

5. No talking. It's a silent game. No hand signals are allowed from classmates.

6. If a rule is broken the teacher can choose to give a warning or reshuffle the cards.

This game is designed to be frustrating. Try to debrief, highlighting the fact that sometimes we take on goals/challenges that are frustrating and hard. It's important to be patient with each other and control emotions. Aim to keep the game light hearted, as sometimes anger towards others can come into play.

Adjust the rules as you see fit. You could do a time challenge, allow non-verbal communication or make it really challenging: even if the numbers are in the correct order, they stay facing down.

The game is about self-control and emotional regulation skills, often key factors in achieving goals. You could have the class set a time target goal.

After the games

In addition to debriefing after you play any of the above games, here are some question ideas you might like to discuss with students:

• What feelings did you notice in yourself? What feelings did you notice in others? Why do you think these feelings came up?

- What skills were needed to be successful in the game? What behaviours made it more challenging?

- What did you learn from the mistakes made during the game?

- What do you think the purpose of the game was?

- How does this game relate to life?

Reward systems

The games described above are just some of the activities and games you can try to keep things interesting.

A good way to make the message stick is to reward students for practising the skills they learn through playing the games.

Educators Kate Chazin and Jennifer Ledford of Vanderbilt University describe rewards as 'a system in which students work individually toward personal reinforcers or work together toward group reinforcers'.

Educator Lucie Renard explains the four benefits to a reward system:

1. *Appropriate behaviour*: When a student is rewarded, they adhere to more appropriate behaviours.

2. *Increased motivation:* Rewards motivate students to participate in more classroom activities.

3. *Joyful students*: When they're more productive, students gain joy through a greater sense of achievement.

4. *Boosted self-esteem*: Rewards can give a student more confidence.

Teacher Cassie of Teach Starter suggests:

Classroom reward systems can be one small part in the mechanics of a positive learning environment. Extrinsic rewards can be used with the aim of being phased out when the rest of your positive learning machine is strong enough to work on its own.

While going about building a strong class, school and home culture, a system that rewards students who demonstrate the class, school or home values can be an effective way to start.

Some of you will already have reward systems in place, whether that be rewarding classroom values, encouraging good behaviour or as a motivator to get work done.

Young people love challenges and find a reward system fun. Often when I run an in-class session, just prior to setting the students a challenge, I'll ask, 'Who likes a challenge?' Generally, 90 per cent of students' hands go straight up.

I recently asked Steven, a year-5 student from Two Wells Primary School, 'Why do you like a reward system?' He responded with, 'Receiving a sticker (or similar) makes me feel proud and it's also encouraging. I find it to be a fun thing we do in the classroom and I am also motivated by it'.

You could recognise your students for demonstrating your class's, school's or home values by:

- presenting students with a certificate
- giving them stickers
- letting them earn badges.

'Badges I can earn'

Here's an example of a reward system I've developed called 'Badges I can earn'. Students work towards being a 'Wellbeing Warrior'. It has been designed as a fun, yet important, way to practise wellbeing skills in the classroom or at home. Students earn the badges by completing all of these 12 tasks:

1. I told someone I appreciate them
2. I helped someone

3. I did something kind

4. I did something hard

5. I forgave someone

6. I kept going even though it was hard

7. I showed empathy

8. I wrote something I am grateful for

9. I exercised

10. I tried something new

11. I invited someone to join in

12. I started a conversation with someone new.

The badges can be used in a few different ways:

- Create a chart with all student or family names on it and print and cut out multiple badges. When a student completes a skill/activity associated with a badge, the appropriate badge gets placed next to the student's name. The aim is to achieve all 12.

- Print and cut out multiple badges. When a student completes a skill/activity associated with a badge, the appropriate badge gets placed in a student health and wellbeing workbook (or similar). The aim is to achieve all 12.

- Display the GWG 'Badges I can earn' poster in the class-room or at home (you'll find the poster in the Resource Pack; see figure 5.7, overleaf). When a student completes a skill/activity associated with a badge, the student has their name entered alongside the badge. The aim is to achieve all 12.

- Create your own ideas. 😊

Figure 5.7: The 'Badges I can earn' poster

The great thing about rewards is that they are also really easy to use at home. This can be done in two ways:

1. Create your own rewards system for the family home. Again, the 'Badges I can earn' challenge is a great place to start.

2. When your child comes home with the reward (sticker, badge or certificate), start a dinner-table conversation about what they did to receive that award.

Be mindful of not overdoing the reward system. As educator Cassie touched on earlier, rewards can be awarded with the aim of being phased out. To avoid overdoing it, you could use the reward system when you are starting out building your wellbeing culture or you could use it as more of an ongoing activity that encourages students to practise wellbeing skills.

Classroom connection

Recently I was playing 'Gratitude Yahtzee' with a year-6 class at Edwardstown Primary School. The students were playing in small groups, we had music filling the room for added energy, there was laughter, there was physical activity involved and the atmosphere in the classroom was full of happy students having fun. It was very satisfying to be a part of. Consider this through the lens of your students.

It's what making wellbeing fun is all about! This is what kids enjoy and love to do, and it cultivates a great connected environment for all involved.

Interestingly, at one year-9 session at Gladstone High School, teacher Luke raised a great point and highlighted exactly why we play games to practise wellbeing and to form connections. He said:

> *When we've asked students to share what they are grateful for in the past, some students didn't like sharing in front of others. But by playing games, the same students were engaged and were able to reflect in a safe and fun way. It also allows for them to share if they like.*

A lot of the activities shared here are ideally suited for students to do by themselves. This is particularly great if you're playing the games with your kids at home. However, encouraging your students to interact with each other in pairs or small groups is an effective method for building connection and a strong classroom community, which is an important element of wellbeing.

Research from Hurst and colleagues suggests that social interaction among/between students in a face-to-face classroom has been shown to promote student learning, increase engagement and build community. Pair and group work can also make it much more fun for students.

So what are some other unique ways we can foster this connection?

The buddy system

One example is through buddy classes. Most schools I have worked with have a buddy class system, where a class in junior primary will be paired with a class in upper primary. This form of interaction lends itself to a perfect opportunity for older students to teach/guide their younger counterparts through some wellbeing practice. And games are a brilliant way to do this.

Some schools use buddy class time to practise wellbeing skills. For example, a year-6 class can be split into small groups. Each group then teaches six to eight year-2 students. The lesson focus is provided (e.g. self/social awareness) but students can be instructed to plan and deliver a 10–15-minute lesson themselves.

This is a great example of wellbeing in action in a buddy class system, but also a great way for the older students to embed their learning, because as we know, one of the best ways to learn is to teach others. Is there a way you could embed wellbeing into your buddy class system?

Interoception rooms

Interoception rooms are becoming more and more popular. These are dedicated rooms where students participate in activities designed to help them connect with their bodies and emotions. Interoception is our eighth sense. It can broadly be defined as our conscious perception of our internal body signals, which let us know how to respond to human needs or relate to our emotional experiences.

To explain how it works and why it's so effective, let's look at the story of Two Wells Primary School, which created an interoception room in 2021. The purpose of the room is to assist students to build self-awareness and self-regulation skills in a fun and engaging way through games and activities. Kurt Ferguson is the Wellbeing for Learning & Engagement Coordinator, and he explains:

Interoception is the pre-requisite for self-regulation. The activities take less than two minutes to complete and they help students to identify their body signals, recognise when their body signals change and act or respond to these body signals for their self-regulation.

Kurt goes on to explain the process:

We start by building understanding of the basic interoceptive skills such as knowing when you're hot and cold, when you need the toilet, tensed vs relaxed muscles; then about the cues for these things in our own body, such as clenched fists and feeling warm may be cues for when you're getting frustrated. Further along in these sessions it does turn to more acting on our self-awareness and regulatory ability and we turn to relationships and interpersonal interactions learning. We do also run some more basic sessions where we teach social skills such as turn-taking, sharing, by-standing behaviours, bullying behaviours, etc. The room is set up for parents to access with their child and the room also doubles up as a space for social and emotional learning.

Two Wells Primary School has now made interoception a part of classroom daily practice. The teacher will start off the day with an interoception activity that doesn't require any equipment. However, if a student is finding it hard to regulate their emotions during the day, they are free to take themselves to the interoception room, which is supervised all the time. Kurt proudly told me that since the room was created they have gone from 320 callouts (the class teacher calling the front office for assistance with behavioural issues) in the first year of the interoception room to just 140 (close to a 70 per cent reduction). This suggests the room is having a tremendous impact on teaching self-awareness and emotional regulation skills. Best of all is that interoception is relevant for everyone. In the resources section at the back of the book, I share a link that provides further detail on interoception rooms and the practice of interoception (see Lean & Leslie 2020).

The South Australian Department for Education describes the benefits of interoception rooms as follows:

- To help children connect to and learn to understand their own bodies and emotions

- To provide children with the tools to know when they are developing emotional reactions and the skills to be in control of those reactions

- Classrooms where interoception is being taught have decreasing behavioural challenges and increased positive wellbeing and prosocial behaviours.

An example of an interoception activity that can be practised in this room goes like this:

- Sitting down with your hands resting on your lap, notice how your hands feel when they are relaxed.

- Now stretch your fingers as wide apart as possible and hold them tense like that for 30 seconds.

- *In what part of your hand could you feel the stretch?*

- We are going to repeat the activity again and when we stretch our fingers, this time we are going to focus on the webs of our fingers.

- Repeat the activity for the second time.

- *How did the webs of your fingers feel? What did you notice?*

Interoception rooms are fun and engaging, particularly for students who struggle with social and emotional learning. The room may not be for all students, but it's highly effective for students who could really use the extra social and emotional skills practice.

Go wild!

The world is your oyster when it comes to games—especially with kids. Don't be afraid to have a go and ask your class for their ideas.

Use your teacher and parent creativity to make wellbeing interaction super fun and engaging, just like wellbeing leader Meagan did at Gilles Street Primary School (see figure 5.8, overleaf).

Figure 5.8: Outdoor Habits of Happiness wheel at Gilles Street Primary

Meagan took the Growing with Gratitude Habits of Happiness wheel and created a version for outdoor student interaction. This is a web app you can use on your classroom smartboard. The teacher or a student presses the 'spin' button and the wheel turns and stops on a number, 1–15. Each number represents an activity. Each class got to choose an activity, which was then added to the wheel. For example, room 4 chose 'Create a fitness circuit in the yard' and room 7 chose 'Think of 3 things you are looking forward to'. A very creative idea for outdoor wellbeing interaction.

The beautiful thing is that the more you encourage greater participation, the more your students will thrive. And it's really easy to carry out these same practices in your home, or at school.

Instead of setting the more traditional academic-based homework tasks, you may like to consider setting wellbeing activities for homework. A game of 'Gratitude Yahtzee' or 'Empathy Basketball' can easily be adapted to the home.

So make time for making fun.

There are more than enough activities, games, tips and tricks in this book for you as a parent to practise wellbeing skills at home with your kids and as a family. As you can see, it doesn't require hours and hours of practice each day—it's more about consistent practice over time.

Better yet, we can get our students to lead these activities for us: that's what we'll look at in the next chapter.

NOW FOR ACTION
Top tip: Early finishers

Include wellbeing time in your classroom by setting up wellbeing activities and games for students who finish their work early (we all have those in our class!).

- You'll find all of the games and activities in this book in the Resource Pack for printing out.

- Store them in a tray labelled 'Wellbeing Games'.

- Introduce the games by playing them as a whole class first, so when it comes to the early finishers accessing them, you won't need to explain the game—they will get straight on with it.

- Pick games such as 'Gratitude Yahtzee', which is easy to start, and then come back to it another time. It's also a game that can be played individually, in pairs or in small groups.

CHAPTER 6
Encourage students to lead

In 2020, Brenton Willson—head of wellbeing at Kilkenny Primary School in Adelaide—and his team set about re-evaluating their school values. But this time things were going to be different. They wanted to build a school culture that was driven by the students—something that hadn't been done before. This led to a set of behaviours that became known as the Caring Agreements.

The Caring Agreements

Brenton explains:

> *Our year 3 to 7s participated in a series of forums. The forums involved students coming up with 10 behaviours they wanted to be embedded at the school.*
>
> *The 10 behaviours that the students came up with are known as the Caring Agreements. We felt this was a brilliant way to hand over ownership and promote a sense of belonging.*

Once the Caring Agreements had been established, they had a competition. Their year 6 and 7 students formed groups of three to four and each group designed a character based on one of the Caring Agreements. They also wrote a short bio on each character, featuring its strengths. The entries were voted on by students and five winners were named. The five winning characters—which they named The Kilkenny Crew—now form their school's values, which are a key part of the school's wellbeing program (see figure 6.1).

Figure 6.1: Student hand-drawn characters of the Kilkenny Crew

The Kilkenny Way

Kilkenny Primary School's wellbeing program is now known as #TheKilkennyWay.

With the five Kilkenny Crew characters and what they represent established, Brenton says the next step was the most powerful one: 'Students, staff and parents worked synergistically to develop the key leadership points that each character is known for'.

Brenton explains how they narrowed down the process:

Hundreds of key statements and words were brainstormed during student/staff/governing council forums. Responses were collated and then fine-tuned with the support of student leaders and then taken to staff. Finally, the responses were taken to the governing council for approval. The descriptions for each agreement and for each of the characters are totally student written with no adult input. The final product underpins all classroom and yard student behaviour management, including students giving the thumbs up to behaviours we like seeing and saying, 'that's the Kilkenny way'. And to the behaviours we don't want to see students put up their hand and say, 'stop, that's not the Kilkenny way'. The final product also underpins restorative processes, as well as behaviour plans, assembly awards and graduation awards. We have a sports day trophy for the team that demonstrates these behaviours best as well.

The Kilkenny Crew

Each of the five Kilkenny Crew characters has a different meaning. Here's how the students chose to describe them.

Pippa the Perseverer

Pippa is brave, stubborn and sometimes a little clumsy. She loves going rock climbing and represents participation: a chance to get involved in things we might never have thought about doing. Remember: the more activities we participate in, the more we will become powerful learners.

Eddie the Elephant

Eddie represents attentive listening, which is listening with your heart, eyes, ears and brain. This is important because when we are listened to attentively, we feel respected and we feel a sense of belonging. We will also learn more.

Perez the Sloth

Perez represents mutual respect. Perez shows kindness to others and helps them. He makes sure his friends are always happy and respects differences. He can be a bit shy at times, but he always tries to be supportive. He does what's right, not what's easy. He might not be the fastest, but he gets things done and has a positive attitude towards everything.

Squirt the Half-Dog, Half-Fish

Squirt will stick by you no matter what. He loves having good friends and he won't judge you for who you are. He knows that it's what's on the inside that counts. Squirt represents appreciation. Appreciation is about being kind, no matter what.

Dave the Donkey

Dave tries his best to overcome his disabilities of having one leg in a cast because he knows he can do anything if he puts his mind to it. He represents 'Only our best will do', which is about trying our best and never giving up. It's about accepting, standing up to new challenges and learning from our mistakes.

* * *

To bring the characters to life, the original drawings were sent off to graphic designer Rodney Love and turned into the very cool cartoon characters of the Kilkenny Crew shown in figure 6.2. (If you visit the school you will see the characters pinned up in all classrooms and around the yard.)

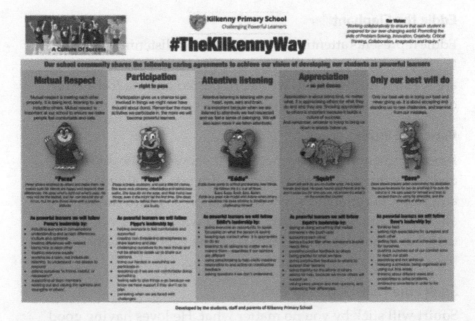

Figure 6.2: The Kilkenny Way poster

The school uses its characters in the following ways:

- *Awards:* Each week, teachers choose two students from their class who displayed the character focus of that week. At the assembly, student leaders read out why the student received the award and present the certificate award to the week's winners.

- *Stickers:* Teachers can reward students for excellent play and learning through Caring Agreement character stickers. This makes the caring agreements visible, and reinforces the behaviours across the school.

- *Prompt of the week:* Each week, the whole school explores a quote based on one of the characters. Teachers can then use discussion questions to promote a dialogue and follow-up action in every class. These are shared with the community through the school's communication app, Dojo, so these discussions can also happen at home.

- *5-day plan:* Reception teacher Jess Pietsch developed a 5-day plan using the Caring Agreements for prep/ kinder/reception and year 1/2 students. The 5-day plan focuses on one of the characters each day. The plan could be used at any time, although the start of the year is ideal to set the learning/behaviour intentions going into the year. Although this example is for junior primary students, you can use your teaching skills to adapt it to any year level, including high school.

Brenton sums this up best when he says, 'Having students name our values added an extra layer of ownership and a sense of belonging'.

A voice of reason

So why is it good to have students create your school's values? First and foremost, it gives students ownership over the values that they want to be part of and follow at their school.

Students also feel a sense of connection and responsibility to the project, as well as each other. This, in turn, helps manage behavioural issues.

In fact, Brenton reported, 'Our staff have noticed a considerable drop in behaviour management, both in the yard and in the classroom'. Brenton goes on to say, 'We believe this has a lot to do with allowing the students to take ownership of the behaviours that they want at our school, giving them a voice'. Student voice matters.

The New South Wales Department of Education describes the importance of student voice as:

- …having students being listened to and heard in different areas of school life.
- …creating consistent opportunities for feedback and reflection [in classrooms]
- …providing ways for students to connect their skills and interests to local community issues and organisations [in community].

I mentioned this earlier in the book, but it's worth highlighting again here. A 2018 executive summary by the Australian Research Council tells us that:

…students view opportunities for meaningful student participation when associated with having influence in school decision making and activities as supporting higher levels of wellbeing. Furthermore, the higher the level of participation, the higher the level of student wellbeing.

In fact, research from Associate Professor Paula Chan suggests that one way to improve student achievement is through supporting student ownership of learning. As students become actively engaged in their learning, they gain a better understanding of their learning targets, how to collect and document evidence of their learning, and how to evaluate and clarify additional learning needs.

And better still: having students lead initiatives can increase their sense of belonging. Sense of belonging is important because it measures a student's perception of being accepted, valued and included in their school setting by their peers and others in the school. A student's sense of belonging is influenced by a complex set of relationships with peers, teachers, families and the broader community.

A student-led approach in education is becoming more and more popular because of the growing body of evidence about its benefits. This approach provides the opportunity for students to 'have a voice' in their school values and their approach to wellbeing, just as Kilkenny Primary has done.

Additionally, promoting wellbeing becomes something the kids want to do instead of something they have to do.

Make the message stick

Of course, setting up values and characters is one thing, but making sure it becomes a self-sustaining cycle is another.

Students at Grange Primary School in Adelaide also developed characters— known as the 'Grangers'—to represent their school values. Senior leader and head of learning, engagement and wellbeing Nick Warren explained how they continue to use and refer to the characters to shape their behaviour management.

For example, Ray the Roo represents 'show respect'. If a student in the yard litters, a teacher or a fellow student will say, 'Are you showing respect to the school by littering?'

Eddie the Emu represents 'best effort', so if the teacher senses a student didn't give their best effort, they will refer to Eddie and ask, 'Are you sure you gave your best effort?'

Here are some other ideas for making the message stick.

Rewards system

Once your students have created your school values, they can be at the forefront of your student rewards system. Awards can be given to students who demonstrate the values in class, at assemblies and even at graduation award ceremonies. You could also have a sports day trophy for the team that best demonstrated the behaviours.

Empowering students

As we all know, giving ownership to students is about empowerment. Research tells us that when educators empower students, they are helping to build their capabilities. Through encouragement, students' confidence can grow and, in turn, they become more optimistic, which also links to action. And this is the power in having students create their own school values: they are more likely to be actioned and adhered to because they belong to the students.

Handing down the baton

Senior students handing down the baton to younger students is about building a strong school culture for years and years to come. Putting the onus on senior students to model the school values in the yard, at school events and in assemblies will go a long way to keeping a strong school culture, based on student-designed values, that can be sustained for the long term. It's also important to allow opportunities for students to model the behaviours. Addressing their peers in the yard, at events and in assemblies provides the perfect opportunity for this. And with your student voice/student wellbeing club in full swing, the foundation is set for the baton to be handed down each year for students to take ownership of the school values.

Class agreements

Building a strong, positive school culture for the long term is also about using the student-led values as your class agreements. This leads to consistency across the school. As we saw, Kilkenny Primary has called these the 'Caring Agreements'. The agreements are displayed in classrooms and around the school, and the teachers model the language when appropriate. And extra points if your wellbeing practice/lessons align with the student-created values.

Making it visible

Don't forget that visibility matters. You might like to display your school's values in the following ways:

- *Banners*: You can display them at school events such as assemblies, sports days and fundraisers, and they can create a conversation point. For example, students can explain to family, friends and visitors what they represent. Imagine how proud it will make them feel!

- *Signs*: Signs can be displayed around the school, outdoors and indoors. They are a highly effective way to remind students of the school's values and they're also a great reminder for teachers and parents. What's more, they also show visitors the school values in an authentic way.

- *Toys (for younger students)*: Having characters made into soft toys is a brilliant way for teachers to tell stories and demonstrate their performing arts skills to model the values. There are some very talented parents out there and you're sure to find one who has soft-toy-making skills.

Alternatively, if you do a google search you're sure to find companies that make customised soft toys. Soft toys can be very comforting for children. You could also consider sending the soft toys home with students on a rotation basis. Doing this can create a strong sense of belonging for students while also teaching them about responsibility.

Use your creativity and tap into your students' creative minds for further ideas.

Get creative

Here's a great example of some students' creative minds at play.

In 2019, I had the pleasure of working with Microsoft Education to create a Growing with Gratitude Minecraft world game. We didn't want to design a game that we assumed students would want to play. We wanted to hand over the ownership to students.

So, we recruited a group of nine students, who were invited to the Microsoft head office in Adelaide (see figure 6.3). Learning Delivery Specialist Steven Payne of Microsoft Education flew over from Perth to help guide the project. As the students entered the room at Microsoft, you could see the excitement on their faces! Steven and I outlined the key skills to include in the game, which included gratitude, kindness, empathy, positive reflection and serving others. We then gave ownership to the students to create a game they would want to play.

The students chose to create a theme-park world. In their world, they included:

- a gratitude rollercoaster ride featuring a gratitude wall activity where students reflect on something in their life that they are grateful for

Figure 6.3: Students at the Microsoft head office, Adelaide

- a vegetable patch (pumpkin) that students reflect on to appreciate the people involved in bringing food to their plate. This includes students creating their own restaurant or kitchen as part of the process

- a kindness maze where, as an act of kindness, students guide a lost sheep out of a maze as a way of practising to be helpful

- a positive reflection zone in which students reflect on the highlights of their theme-park experience.

Providing opportunities for students to lead is a powerful way to ensure a strong wellbeing program.

They also included a designated zone (with instructions) where other students playing the game can design their own part of the theme park.

I witnessed the power in giving ownership to students first hand. I overheard one of the girls telling her teacher, 'This is the best day of my life'. The confidence and pride the students walked away with was mind blowing. They also took away the satisfaction in knowing students from potentially all over the world would play the game they designed to practise gratitude and other key wellbeing skills. Providing opportunities for students to lead is a powerful way to ensure a strong wellbeing program.

Lead by example

In chapter 2, I spoke about the importance of forming a student voice group to promote wellbeing across your school. It's about allowing students ownership when it comes to wellbeing at school.

The student voice group's (or student wellbeing club's) role is to come together once a fortnight or once a month (whatever works for you) to represent their fellow students and to create initiatives themselves in the wellbeing space. Scotch College Adelaide has named its group/club 'The Student Action Team'.

Shawn Kasbergen, Director of Student Wellbeing at Scotch, explains: 'A critical component in the success of our wellbeing programs has been the inclusion of Student Action Team leaders across both our junior and senior school campuses'. Each year, the team is tasked with making wellbeing principles 'actionable' and 'doable' for the student cohort. Shawn goes onto say, 'These key structures include year-6 action teams structured around our Pillars of the Live Well program, which runs from years 5 to 9'.

The pillars include sustainable living, food technology and nutrition, physical wellbeing, wellbeing and values education, global responsibility and service learning. Students have an exciting series of events and challenges in place. Activities include the ever-popular 21-day challenges, which focus on nutrition, sleep, language, gratitude, procrastination and mental health.

As an example, the college's 21-day gratitude challenge looks like this:

- a launch by the Student Wellbeing Action Team leader at assembly

- regular emails from the Student Action Team leader about the why and how of gratitude

- daily gratitude journaling, where students write three things each day that they are grateful for. They are encouraged to pin them up at home as a reminder of the good things and to disrupt negativity bias

- a 'Power of Gratitude' focus session during mentor time featuring definitions and prompts like the one from Soul Pancake (check out the resources section at the back of the book for a link to their video)

- an invitation to write a gratitude letter and to subsequently give it to a friend, teacher, parent, grandparent, coach, tutor or someone else

- gratitude boards, where students place a leaf on a gratitude tree; the leaf mentions something they are grateful for

- students are given the opportunity to write a gratitude letter to a teacher, which is then packaged up and delivered to their pigeon hole on World Teacher Day.

Encouraging and providing the opportunities for your students to lead is a tremendous way to help create a strong and robust wellbeing program across your school for the long term.

The great news is that you can also encourage your kids to lead at home. This could involve having them create family challenges, design a personal character based on a strength or a value they want to be known for or create an award for family members who demonstrate your home values. They could also be responsible for setting up a wellbeing wall: a display wall in your home that could feature a gratitude space, quote posters or wellbeing frameworks (there are more ideas in the Resource Pack for you to access).

Let's allow our students to lead!

And finally, let's not forget we need to lead by example. We'll delve into that in the next chapter.

NOW FOR ACTION
What do you value?

As a school leader or teacher, or as a parent, consider the following questions:

- Do you know your school's values?
- Do you know the history behind the values and who created them?
- Are they ever referred to? Or are they there to tick a box?
- Are they visible?
- Do you have a character that represents each value?
- Are the values due to be reviewed?
- Do you see benefit in having students take ownership of the school values? If so, what's the first step you can take to make this happen?

If your school is going through the process or not quite ready to have students take ownership of the school values, you could take the lead and have students create your class or year level values using the methods described in this chapter. And why not create family values and characters to match at home?

CHAPTER 7
Manage your own wellbeing

I'm confident we'd all agree that looking after kids is bloody hard work!

Whether you're a teacher, a parent, a youth worker, a principal, a caregiver, a junior sports coach... You're dealing with complex emotions, behaviour, COVID-19 protocols, pressures of standardised testing, and the list goes on... And these challenges occur on a daily basis.

Just like any role or responsibility, it's really easy to get lost in the day to day, to put everyone else's needs before your own. That's why it's really important to look after your own mental health and wellbeing.

Whatever your role—as a teacher, educator, parent or caregiver—you're unable to support the mental wellbeing of young people trusted in your care unless you're looking after your own wellbeing first and foremost.

But for most of us, that's an issue in itself. Here's why.

The stats say it all

According to the National Foundation for Educational Research, teaching is one of the most stressful jobs in the world. That's quite alarming—although maybe not that surprising, right?

In fact, research conducted by Donna Cross of the University of Western Australia titled 'Teacher Wellbeing and its Impact on Student Learning' revealed that there are key issues teachers in Australia, the UK, New Zealand and the United States report they are facing:

- high workloads

- workplace bullying

- poor leadership

- time-management issues

- expectations of new teachers to produce the same results as experienced teachers

- high expectations from parents

- high expectations from standardised testing

- having hard conversations with students, parents, colleagues and school leaders

- being under appreciated

- being underpaid.

What's more, a 2021 Australian College of Education survey of more than 500 Australian teachers revealed that:

- 84 per cent of educators were considering a career change

- 75 per cent feel stressed by their work

- 82 per cent struggle with work–life balance

- 36 per cent are not satisfied in their job.

- 26 per cent are working at least six days a week
- 49 per cent are dissatisfied with their pay.

Now, while I count myself lucky that I wouldn't usually include myself in these statistics, there's something else not represented here that's even more worrying.

The root of the problem

During 2015, while working as a primary-school teacher, I spent the majority of days turning up to school anxious and trying to hide it. My mental wellbeing issues had nothing to do with my role at school—they were more to do with a personal breakup I was going through—but they definitely impacted my ability to lead our PE department.

I had to withdraw myself from our shared office regularly because I couldn't bear the thought of talking with people. This had nothing to do with my colleagues or the school. For the first time I felt a sense of loneliness and a lack of self-worth, and I developed severe anxiety.

One Sunday I was in bed, not wanting to face the world, and I didn't know how I was going to get through the coming week at school. I felt my only option was to take some time off, so I booked a doctor's appointment. Even though it was a simple task, it felt like a mammoth effort to make the appointment.

After being called into the doctor's small consultation room, I sat down with the anxiety butterflies kicking in my stomach. The doctor asked, 'How can I help?' Not being able to make eye contact, my eyes just looked to his shoes and, while fighting back tears, I responded with, 'I am going through a tough time. I think I need some time off work, but I'm too embarrassed to let my employer know the reason'. The doctor showed empathy and said, 'No problem, I'll write you a medical certificate'. A sense of relief came over me, but the anxiety remained.

I didn't want to go down the anti-depressant path, as I believed it wasn't the right solution for me. It had been more than five years since I had started my consistent practice of gratitude and positive reflection, so I made the decision to 'pop gratitude' and other positive actions, instead of 'popping pills'.

I returned to adopting many of the skills and practices we've already discussed in this book. I focused on gratitude, empathy and positive reflection to reframe things to a more positive point of view. I started serving others and volunteering (which I'll get to in a moment) because it took the focus off me and moved it to a greater purpose.

This was not an overnight solution to my anxiety, lack of self-worth and loneliness. But, after three months of consistent practice, I got myself back to a neutral state where I felt the anxiety subside. I began to connect with friends again and my self-esteem improved. It wasn't a sprint solution—it was more of a marathon—but 'popping gratitude' and the other positive habits is what helped me move forward from my biggest challenge as an adult.

I know I'm not the only person who has experienced something like this because at the end of the day—parents, teachers, or whatever our role is—we're human! And whatever is going on at home will impact work, and vice versa. We aren't immune!

I feel as educators and parents we all have the responsibility to role model gratitude, physical activity, empathy, kindness, positive reflection, service and self-awareness skills.

Two central skills

Through positive education, we are helping to 'build and protect' the mental wellbeing of ourselves and the young people in our care.

So, when we are going through a challenging time, we have two very important skills to draw on:

1. *self-awareness:* Self-awareness can be broadly defined as the extent to which people are consciously aware of their internal states and their interactions or relationships with others.

    Self-awareness of our mental wellbeing is powerful: it gives us the ability to understand how we're feeling. These feelings could be positive emotions such as pure joy and happiness. You could experience these emotions through a big breakthrough in the classroom or by achieving something meaningful to you. Or it could be negative emotions such as frustration, stress or sadness. You could have had a run-in with a parent or be stressed in your personal life.

    It's worthy of mentioning that there's nothing wrong with experiencing negative emotions: we're human beings and it's going to happen. Being self-aware is the first step. Say to yourself, *I am not coping at the moment as well as I'd like. I am not feeling my best and I need to seek some support or help.*

2. *ownership:* One of my favourite books of all time is *Extreme Ownership* by retired Navy Seal Jocko Willink. Jocko says that 'there is no-one else to blame; you must own your problems along with solutions'.

I've had many conversations with teachers over the years, and a common theme emerges from these discussions: *Teaching can be a demanding and stressful role. Some days I handle the stress better than others, but at the end of the day, it's really up to me to be responsible for my own wellbeing.*

It's true that the environment you work in can, and should, support your wellbeing, but it is also your individual responsibility.

It's critical that as school leaders, teachers, parents, caregivers and youth workers, we recognise where we are at and what we are feeling, and reach out for help or support when we need it most.

Prioritise you

Now, remember that I'm not a GP, psychologist or health professional, but I do recommend that you seek out the kind of support you need, and don't feel embarrassed or ashamed for doing so because that's your duty as a role model! (There are some great contacts in the resources section at the back of the book to help you.)

On a day-to-day basis, however, there are some practices that I have personally adopted to help me in tough times, many of which I've touched on in this book. I'd like to share a couple more here, just to encourage you to adopt your own regular wellbeing practice at home.

These are just suggestions: feel free to play around with them and come up with your own practices. Remember: we are role models and our kids will always benefit from seeing us put these things into practice.

OVER TO YOU
Gratitude journal

Okay, this might seem counterintuitive because I mentioned previously that our kids find journaling about what we're grateful for every day quite boring — but hear me out.

Keeping a diary where you write one to three things you're grateful for each day is a great starting point. Over time, this practice may become a chore, so mix it up, get creative and get your family involved.

I recently had a conversation with a great mate, Jarrad, who has four-year-old twin boys. He asks his boys every night at bedtime what they are grateful for. He shared: 'The boys just love it and at bedtime they ask if they can do the gratitude practice. The other night one of the boys said, "I am grateful for Dad's cuddles because it makes me feel good"'. (Now there's a win–win.)

Dump it down

There's power in writing down how you're feeling, rather than having it bottled up in your mind. This style of journaling can help with clarity.

I like to grab a coffee on a Sunday morning and spend 10–15 minutes just writing down my thoughts. I invest in a nice blank notepad for this and it makes the experience something I truly look forward to.

Here are some ideas to guide you in your weekly reflection. In a notepad, write down:

- how you're feeling
- what's bothering you
- what's going well
- what you want to work on
- what action you can take to make a change.

(continued)

Daily positive reflection

Can you think of a day where a number of fantastic things happened and one or two that were not so good? What did you focus on the most?

If you're like most of us, it's likely it was one of the negative experiences. As humans beings, we're wired to focus on the negatives (remember, this is known as our 'negativity bias', which we addressed in chapter 4).

However, the great new is, we can train our brain to focus on the positives. Psychologist and neuroscience expert Dr Rick Hanson is famous for saying, 'Neurons that fire together, wire together'.

Here's a powerful way to train your brain to fire up and focus on the positives.

Spend one minute writing down one thing you

- are grateful for.
- did for someone else.
- did to add value to your life.
- are looking forward to.

You could keep a notepad next to your bed and just before going to sleep complete the exercise. It's a great way to 'habit stack' (which I talked about in chapter 3). The habit already developed is going to bed and you're adding the daily positive reflection to the existing habit.

Serve others

In 2015, I came across a quote from the 14th Dalai Lama, Tenzin Gyatso. He says:

> *When you care for others, you manifest an inner strength despite any difficulties you face. Your own problems will seem*

less significant and bothersome to you. Reaching beyond your own problems and taking care of others, you gain confidence, courage and a greater sense of calm.

Reading this was powerful, and the timing was perfect because I was in a bad place mentally. I immediately searched for volunteering opportunities so I could be of service to something bigger than myself. It was Muhammad Ali who said, 'Service to others is the rent you pay for your room here on earth'. This is one of my favourite quotes.

After googling 'volunteering Adelaide', I came across Fred's Van. I was aware of Fred's Van, but I didn't really know its purpose. I soon learned that it's a service overseen by St Vinnies. Fred's Van is a food service for people who are experiencing homelessness or are at risk of homelessness and marginalisation. There are vans that travel around to different areas, as well as community centre locations.

So, every third Thursday of the month since 2015 I've been volunteering at Fred's Van at the Kilburn Community Centre in South Australia.

On my very first evening, three things stood out:

1. Volunteering at an organisation that serves homeless/ vulnerable people helped put things in perspective immediately.

2. It helped to give me a sense of purpose.

3. It took my mind off my own problems and onto something that was far greater than myself.

Research from Martin Binder and Andreas Freytag suggests that people with lower levels of mental wellbeing can get a bigger boost from volunteering, compared to people who already have a reasonable sense of happiness in their life.

I have personally found volunteering to be a great way to serve and contribute to the wider community. And the other significant benefit is the positive impact it has on my own mental wellbeing.

I continue to volunteer every third Thursday of the month. Our volunteer team has built a strong community; we are a part of something bigger than ourselves, and we have a blast. But, most importantly, we are making a small difference in people's lives and it's something we all look forward to each month.

I'd highly recommend giving it a go if you're looking to add purpose and happiness to your life, while making a difference. Ideas for volunteering include:

- food service (soup kitchen, food bank)
- community gardener
- laundry service
- youth work (drop-in centres, 1:1 support)
- animal shelter
- sports coach
- team manager
- read to the elderly
- chat to the elderly
- leisure buddy (building relationships with adults with intellectual disabilities)
- op-shop assistant.

The great thing about volunteering is it doesn't have to be just focused on you. You could search for opportunities to volunteer as a family, and at school you could provide opportunities for students to volunteer at events—such as fundraisers or junior sports days—or perhaps in the wider community. I have accompanied students to retirement homes, Ronald

McDonald House and community fun runs, where students have volunteered.

To find many more volunteering opportunities in Australia you could start by looking at the Go Volunteer website.

Three easy ways to shift your mood

Our wellbeing is a serious topic and shouldn't just be fixed by mood enhancers provided by a doctor. We should definitely look for 'mood shifters' on a day-to-day basis. They are easy and free ways to improve our mood straight away.

These are not necessarily prescribed by a professional (although maybe they should be!). They are long-term strategies that you can use all the time and they are things you can practise on your own, with kids or with others.

Here are three mood shifters that research from Szabo and Eerola tell us are ways to improve our mood (particularly when we're having a tough time). I'd love to challenge you to do all three in the next 24 hours!

1. Physical activity

    Go for a short walk around the block or move around instead of staying stationary on yard duty. We are not designed to be sedentary beings! Dopamine and happy hormones flood our body when we are active. It could be a walk, a jog or a home workout. There are heaps of free home workouts available online that require very little equipment. My favourite is a high intensity interval training (HIIT) class. It's challenging, but I always walk out feeling a million dollars; it's the best medicine for mental wellbeing that I have found. Think of ways you can add a little more movement to your day, and get the kids involved: they will never say no to a bit of movement!

You could take your students out for a fun game or even give them some sporting equipment and allow them to have free play.

2. Music

    Crank up your favourite song in the living room or car and go nuts. Or combine music with physical activity: pop on your headphones and go for a walk or run. Listening to your favourite songs is a sure way to lift your mood. Keep your favourites on a 'Happy mood' playlist.

    You could also play music (when appropriate) in class. Wellbeing lesson time could be an opportunity.

3. Laughter

    How good is it to have a good old solid belly laugh? Kids are naturally the best at cracking jokes and being silly. There is a reason why 'funny cats' is one of the most searched terms on YouTube. One workshop participant of mine admitted he found YouTube videos of little kids toppling over while learning to walk hilarious. There are also funny memes or GIFs out there that could send you into hysterics.

    Or you could introduce a joke of the day in your class or play a funny video clip of cats and dogs playing up.

For me, if I'm having a bad day, I'm now self-aware that physical activity and gratitude are the main two things that help improve my mood. However, what works for me, may not work for you, so it's important to experiment to find your 'mood shifters'.

And you don't need to wait until you're in a bad mood to perform your mood shifters. It's important to also practise them when you're feeling good so you can give yourself an extra boost of happiness — and, like I said, kids love getting involved in this stuff!

There are other ways, too, we can look at including these kinds of practices as a staff group, or as a whole school. Let's look at these now.

Wellbeing in staff meetings

It's no joke that staff meetings can be boring. We've all been in one where that one person just talks for the sake of it, repeats themselves 12 times, repeats what someone else has said and, just as you think the staff meeting is over, they start again.

However, despite this often painful experience, staff meetings actually provide an opportunity to create good habits and practices. Staff meetings are a consistent event that is a requirement and therefore presents the perfect opportunity for staff wellbeing practices.

OVER TO YOU

Here are four activities you could rotate through, across your school year, to include in every staff meeting.

1. Wellbeing check-in

The wellbeing check-in is an impactful way to allow staff to practise self-awareness and it's also a terrific way to begin staff meetings. I love starting any staff training with this.

There are two stages to this exercise.

Stage 1: Rate yourself

First, ask participants to rate their mood on the wellbeing check-in scale, which you can present on your staffroom screen (it's available in the Resource Pack; see figure 7.1, overleaf)

(continued)

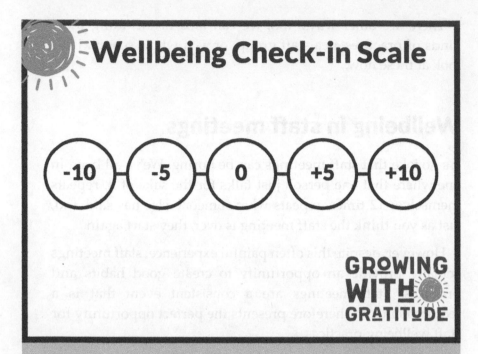

Figure 7.1: Wellbeing check-in scale

It's important to describe the scale numbering so staff members accurately identify their feelings. Tell them:

- –10 = you probably shouldn't be here because you're dealing with some kind of tragedy or you are going through a really hard time in your life.

- –5 = you could be having a rough day, where something happened or a chain of events occurred that have put you in a bad mood. Or maybe you're thinking 'Who's this guy coming in to talk about positive education?' and it's put you in a bad mood (my idea of attempted humour, with the aim of getting a few chuckles).

- 0 = I'm okay; things aren't too bad. A neutral state.

- +5 = I'm feeling really good. I had a great day; my class participated really well; I'm feeling in a positive frame of mind.

- +10 = Well, things could not be better. I had the best day; I walked into the room giving out high fives at will and I'm in a fantastic mood.

Next, I play a four-minute clip of a hilarious prank call Aussie comedy duo Hamish and Andy performed live on air. Hamish calls a random phone number and asks the guy on the other end if he could be a reference for a job interview that Hamish is about to go into. Hamish explains he doubts he'll get a call, but just in case. The guy agrees. Well, you guessed it: he gets a call (Andy calls him) and does his utmost to be the best referee for Hamish. The purpose of playing the funny video is that laughter improves our mood and it also increases the energy in the room after a long day of teaching. (For a giggle, google 'Hamish and Andy prank call' on YouTube).

Once the video has finished, I have participants check back in to see if their mood has improved after laughing or even just smiling. The vast majority of the time, they report an increase in mood, even it's only one or two numbers forward.

It's also important to highlight that it's hard to go from −5 to +5 within a couple of minutes, but you may well find you go from −3 to 0; and from that more neutral state, you can work your way up to the positive numbers.

Stage 2: Shift the mood

Once they know how they're currently feeling, it's time to shift the mood of the group!

As I described earlier, music, physical activity and laugher are three proven ways to shift our mood.

As a group, you've just practised laughter, so encourage your staff to try music and physical activity; even better, why not play music in the staff meeting when appropriate? When staff are discussing ideas or working in teams, why not provide the option for them to walk and talk? It's a great way to involve physical activity.

(continued)

The mood shifter activity could be the way you start all staff meetings.

But you don't have to play a funny video every time: a connection game is also an effective way to start a meeting on a positive note. A connection game is a fun activity (similar to an icebreaker activity) that gets people moving and laughing and helps to create psychological safety (google 'connection games' for ideas). Observe the energy in the room when you do your mood-shifter activity: it's likely there will be a lift in energy throughout the room. You can also use this activity in the classroom and at home.

2. Gratitude wall/jar

A great activity for staff is to create a staffroom gratitude wall and/or gratitude jar. The purpose of the wall/jar is they both provide a visual representation and a place to store the blessings in our lives. It's also an activity that helps to build a strong culture of gratitude among staff.

It works like this:

- Have a stack of sticky notes (gratitude wall) or a pile of small, pre-cut coloured paper (gratitude jar) sitting near the wall/jar.

- As staff members walk into the staffroom for the start of a meeting, encourage them to write down on a piece a paper/ sticky note a gratitude reflection.

- Instead of staff generally reflecting on what they are grateful for, you could display a question on the whiteboard/ smartboard. For example: *What was something about your day that made you grateful?* Next time, the reflection could be, *What can you see in the staffroom that you are grateful for?*

- Introduce the gratitude wall or jar at a staff meeting. Explain the concept to staff members and tell them that at the beginning of each meeting, they will be asked to write a gratitude reflection as they enter the room.

The other benefit of having a permanent gratitude wall or jar is that staff can practise their gratitude whenever they like.

3. Positive reflection

The purpose of the positive reflection activity is for staff to reflect on the positives from their day and across the week. As we know, teaching can be stressful, but there are always good things to focus on, so let's train our brains to focus on the good.

It works like this:

Allocate 5 minutes to reflect on these questions:

- What was the best part of your day?
- What are one to three things you did for someone else?
- What are one to three things you did to add value to your life?
- What's something you are looking forward to?

When introducing the positive reflection routine, spend a few minutes at a staff meeting explaining the concept and that it will be a regular feature at your staff meetings.

Over time, observe the shift in positivity among staff. Staffrooms have a reputation for being a very negative environment!

4. The boundary of belonging

I've never met anyone who doesn't want to feel they belong. However, there could be times when we feel like we're an outsider. 'The boundary of belonging' is one of the most powerful activities you can participate in as a way of understanding this and also building the empathy muscle.

'The boundary of belonging' has been adapted from Simon Sinek's book, *Leaders Eat Last*. It's a great activity to do at the start of the school year or at the start of a school term. You could aim to do the activity once per term because it's so powerful.

I've actually done the activity with students and staff. In fact, I've even done a version of the activity with 5-year-olds in student

(continued)

leadership sessions (where older students assist younger ones). It can also be adapted to do at home.

Note: it's best to use PowerPoint because you will need to reveal the boundary of belonging in sections. You can access the PowerPoint in the Resource Pack. Here's an edited version of the activity.

Step 1

Show teachers the boundary of belonging on your laptop or screen.

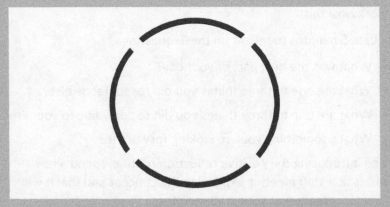

Step 2

Ask, 'Is it fair to say that everyone wants to come to [insert school's name] and to feel like they belong: that they want to be included and to be happy?' You will likely have nods of agreement and comments of 'yes'.

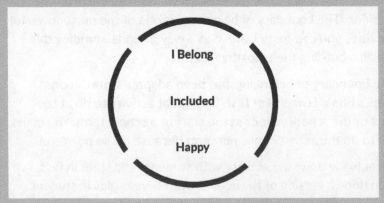

Step 3

- Continue with, 'However, there could be times when you feel like you don't belong. You could feel excluded or feel unhappy'.

- Ask, 'What could happen to make you feel that way?'

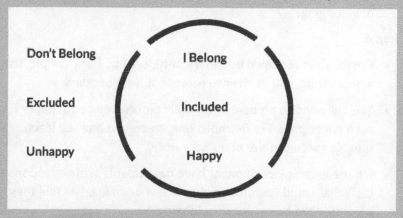

Step 4

Before revealing the next part of the slide (empathy), you could say, 'We agreed before that everybody wants to belong, feel included and feel happy here at [insert school's name]. Now, this comes down to one thing and that is empathy (click to reveal the arrow and the word 'empathy').

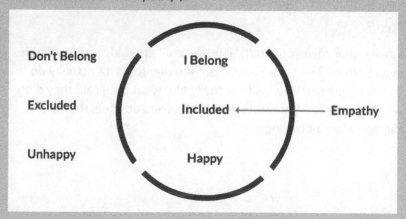

(continued)

Step 5

- Next, facilitate a group discussion on 'What is empathy?'
- Continue the group discussion by asking, 'What could you do to make sure your colleagues feel they are inside the boundary of belonging?'

Step 6

- Create your very own boundary of belonging. For example, use a hoop, rope, mat or chair to represent the boundary.
- You will need to prepare two small coloured pieces of paper for each participant. For example: one green and one red (each roughly twice the size of a sticky note).
- On the green piece of paper have participants write a response to: 'What could you do to make sure your colleagues feel they are inside the boundary of belonging?'
- And on the red piece of paper have participants write a response to: 'How might your colleagues feel excluded, unhappy or that they don't belong?'
- Have staff place the green paper inside the boundary and the red one outside the boundary.
- Read a few responses back to the group.

Step 7

Finally, challenge your staff: 'These are all great ideas, but what is even better?' The response you are looking for is 'to actually do it'. Challenge participants to actually 'do' what they said they'd do within the next 24 hours, to help make someone feel they are in the boundary of belonging.

Be Good to Yourself Day

It could be time for school leaders and governing councils to consider allowing teachers to take a mental wellbeing day off at least once a year or perhaps once a term. Swiss International Scientific School in Dubai allows staff to take a day off a year, whenever they choose to, as part of their staff wellbeing program. They call this initiative 'Be Good to Yourself Day'.

Sharing resources at school

I was running a staff training session at Gilles Street Primary School at the start of the year before students returned. The topic turned to staff wellbeing and, as we know, workload is one of the stresses teachers face—especially planning lessons and creating resources. I asked, 'Who has a system where you share lesson plans and resources?' No-one put their hand up. So Principal Michael Bawden said, 'Ash, you make a great point. Let's add this onto our agenda for this afternoon'.

Sharing resources across your year level team, and even a year level above or below, is a wonderful way to reduce your workload. It also builds a sense of community. Another option is, for example, if you have a passion for maths and another teacher who teaches the same year level has a passion for health, why not swap your lesson plans, materials or resources? You've just halved your planning time!

You could use a platform such as Google Drive, Dropbox or an internal system at your school. To take it a step further, you could start a Facebook group where teachers from all around the world share lesson plans and resources.

You could also consider a teacher buddy system, particularly to support new teachers to the school. It's a simple concept of pairing a new teacher at the school with an existing teacher. It's an effective way of supporting new teachers, whether that be with resources or helping them learn systems and protocols. Simple and easily actionable—just like all the other tips and tools I've armed you with in this chapter!

But remember, it's wonderful to have the intention to practise wellbeing skills, but this means nothing unless you act on it. And as self-help guru Tony Robbins once said, 'Gratitude is useless, unless you practise'.

So, let's get practising today and make gratitude a part of who we are, so we can encourage it in our kids.

NOW FOR ACTION
Self check-in

Rate how you're currently feeling:

- –10 = not in a great place at all

- 0 = neutral: 'I'm okay; things aren't too bad'

- +10 = things couldn't be better

- everything in between.

  -10   -5   0   +5   +10

Self-awareness

Why do you feel you're at this number?

Ownership

What's your mood shifter? If you feel you're in the minuses or even in the pluses, what can you do to improve your mood? For example, physical activity, music, laughter or something else from this book, such as writing a letter of thanks to someone you love or surprising a colleague with a small gift.

Positive reflection

What have you got coming up that you're looking forward to?

Now act! Go and do something that improves your mood — and get your kids involved too!

THE FUTURE IS NOW

In 2015, teachers Desy Pantelos and Teresa Marshall attended a four-day positive education training session facilitated by Geelong Grammar in Victoria. With many learnings and light-bulb moments over the four days, Desy and Teresa returned to Kidman Park Primary School in South Australia enthused and with an innovative vision. They were on a mission, bustling through the school gates, desperate to get to Principal John Clarke's office to pitch him their idea.

Desy pretty much knocked down John's door, yelling 'John, we must make positive education a specialist lesson!'

Prior to his days as school principal, John worked in correctional services and remains keenly involved in scouts. This experience led him on the path to understand the importance of social and emotional learning. So, John was all ears.

Desy and Teresa's idea was to make positive education a specialist lesson, like physical education, music, art and languages are. This would involve setting up a positive education classroom, and each class in the school would come to Desy once a week for a positive education lesson. Their plan was to also support classroom teachers with resources that they could use to implement wellbeing in their classroom. Desy bought buckets for each class that she filled regularly with resources (some are also shared digitally).

Desy explains:

Providing additional resources for class teachers reinforces what the students are learning in my lessons and it provides more opportunities for students to practise. One special lesson a week is great, but it's not enough to build consistency.

Now, to some of you this idea might sound simplistic, and to others it could be completely batty! But Principal John believed social and emotional learning required explicit teaching and a consistent approach, so he was willing to give it a go.

The next step was to get approval from the school's governing council. So Desy and her team pitched the proposal. The presentation included the purpose behind positive education and, most importantly, how it would benefit the students. The governing council were on board. However, to be realistic there had to be a trade-off.

An existing specialist subject needed to be dropped so the timetables didn't become too cramped. The school leadership team decided it would be art. However, as art and creativity are important, Desy committed to including art projects in her positive education lessons. The class teachers also added art to their timetables. Everyone was a winner!

It didn't take long for the governing council to approve the inclusion of positive education as a specialist subject at the school. In fact, the idea was met with a sense of excitement and enthusiasm.

So, in 2015, positive education became a specialist subject at Kidman Park Primary School.

The school even set up a dedicated classroom for the weekly 45-minute lesson. They named it 'The PEARL Room':

- P = Positive
- E = Education

- A = Assists
- R = Real
- L = Life Skills.

Naming the room gave the students a sense of community and commonality. Desy shares:

I have former students who are now in high school who come and visit and talk about how they miss coming to the PEARL room. They say, 'Now I understand what you meant when you taught us things like compassion'.

This reflection from past students is important for us on the forefront of change. You may never really know the impact you have on your students that they take into adulthood. You may **We need to think of the future, and of the future of our next generation.** not witness the impact of the positive education program immediately. As historian Henry B Adams said, 'A teacher affects eternity; he can never tell where his influence stops'.

We need to think of the future, and of the future of our next generation.

The reason why this example in particular is important, and why I share it here at the conclusion of the book, is because if we want to have any hope of helping our next generation become resilient and be able to adapt to all the changes and complexities that life throws at them, we need to come up with innovative solutions that show them the importance of this and also practise what we preach. We need to think of the future, and of the future of our next generation.

Practise what we preach

Wellbeing and resilience are now coming of age in education. This field has the potential to make a significant contribution to how teaching and learning are conceptualised within the next decade to create more resilient, robust and flourishing education systems in which all young people believe they belong.

The 2020 pandemic is a great example of the tumultuous times we now live in. As Professor of Education Leadership Alma Harris argues in a publication titled *Wellbeing and Resilience Education about COVID-19 and its Impact on Education*:

> *As the severity of pandemic impact ... flows through societies across the world, school leaders and teachers may believe they are returning to a new normal. As ... equilibrium returns, we contend that what is unfolding ... will mean we are not at the same point in the change cycle.*

It's a fair argument to suggest resilience is the future of education. As someone at the forefront of education, it's likely you agree too.

However, to make it happen requires action, like the action that Desy, Teresa and Kidman Park Primary took.

Being an educator, a school leader, a principal or a parent means you now have this amazing opportunity to create an environment that supports our young people to practise adaptable thinking and emotional regulation skills.

You and the staff at your school can achieve this by setting up a strong, robust whole-school approach to positive education and wellbeing, and leaving a legacy for future generations. It's up to us to be proactive. It's up to us to lead and drive the change.

So, while having a positive education program as a specialist subject that is integrated into the whole school might seem like something out of reach or a bit futuristic, the example from Kidman Park Primary shows it can be done. I haven't come across many other schools that do wellbeing this way—yet—but I have mentioned in this book the ones that I have found. For me, these examples are the future of education.

We owe it to ourselves and our children to think ahead.

If you still need a reminder of why we must act now, remember these three things.

- Improved academic achievement
  Research from the Institute of Positive Education at Geelong Grammar suggests that social and emotional practices in schools can increase academic achievement, particularly when practices focus on building skills that lead to greater resilience, such as gratitude, empathy and kindness.

  In addition, recent research from the Australian National University of 3400 15-year-olds found that self-reported levels of depression had a large, negative effect on their National Assessment Program—Literacy and Numeracy (NAPLAN) results months later.

- Increased resilience

  Through consistent practice of social and emotional skills, we are helping young people to develop their resilience muscle by building up their inner strength to work through stress and challenges that may arise.

- Better emotional regulation/reframing skills

  Students learn how to use their self-talk to see a negative situation from a more positive perspective. This isn't an easy skill to learn, but through consistent practice and modelling it's one of the most useful and important skills a human being can possess.

And don't just take my word for it. I'd like to leave you with some reflections from real students from Kidman Park Primary School that aptly show what we're setting up our future for.

Every day of my life I was grateful about everything. My life was perfect because I have a roof over my head, and loving and good supportive friends. Then on the third of April 2016 everything changed.

My mum and dad took me to the hospital because I had symptoms of type 1 diabetes, and when the doctors tested my blood it was confirmed. When I asked them if there was a cure they said there was no cure at all and I have to live with it for the rest of my life.

After that, the nurses said I have to take insulin injections three or four times a day with five blood tests. I had to stay in hospital for one week and I felt like I didn't want to live anymore because of all the needles and blood tests every single day, and the first thing I have to do when I wake up was an injection and even before I sleep.

My first few injections at the hospital hurt so much and I felt upset that every night I had tears going down my eyes. When I returned to school I wasn't my cheerful self anymore, but on every Thursday in between recess and lunch we have PEARL and Mrs Pantelos teaches us how to meditate and how to have gratitude. If it wasn't for these lessons, Mrs Pantelos and my family I wouldn't have been happy.

Kidman Park, Year 7 student

* * *

For most of my life, there's always been bad moments. Like when dad left when I was not even a year old, I could just walk. My mum has been in hospital lots of times. Sometimes I'd wait for her for a week, sometimes even 3 months. There would mainly be arguments in the family, and I would end up in my room, door locked and blinded by tears.

For all these years I had no solution for how to be calm and more positive, and to me, the only people that were positive a lot of the time were my mum and aunties, this was before me and my friends matured. That was until the teachers were talking about how art would be replaced with Positive ED.

At first I never tried the new subject. My first lesson of PEARL came and I felt a little better. As the lessons carried on I began to feel better. Bad things still commonly happen, but I am still on my feet. And for that … that is why I've continued to study, keep up with my work, and still kept friends. Heck, I still have a friend from Kindergarten. PEARL, to me, is probably my favourite thing to do at school. Whenever I come into the classroom and I see that it's Thursday, a little voice in my head is cheering, and I know that it will be the highlight to my day.

Kidman Park, Year 7 student

GRATITUDE

I know this is the last part of the book, but it's probably the most important. After all, I've spent a great deal of this book talking about how we have to practise what we preach! So here goes …

To all the people who have supported me on my journey in writing this book, and those people who gave their time for interviews: you are all greatly appreciated and I'd like to acknowledge each of you now.

First of all, thank you to my mum, Bev, and dad, Mark. Growing up you gave Toni and me every opportunity to pursue our dreams. You were up early driving me to cricket, basketball and football for well over a decade. You were always encouraging and I have no doubt this encouragement has resulted in me going all in with Growing with Gratitude. Mum, you are the kindest and most caring person I know. I don't recall you telling us to be kind, but you taught us in the most powerful way and that's by showing us through your example. I am aware I am a fair way off your level of kindness, but it's a skill that I work on and will continue to. I love you both very much.

To my sister Toni, brother in-law Bjorn and nephews Coop and Ed. Your ongoing support is greatly appreciated. Love you all.

To my grandparents, Papa Bill, Nana Bobbie, Gramps Ken and Nana June: growing up, you demonstrated kindness, what it meant to serve others, humour, work ethic and love. I didn't realise it at the time, but now I see what you demonstrated is a huge part of what this book is about. I remember calling you (Nana Bobbie) 'Bobbie' when I was seven, complaining because I'd been told off by mum, but as always, you had my back and you were on my side. Rest in peace Bill, Bobbie and Ken. Nana June: keep going (94 not out).

To all my cousins, aunties and uncles: you are all so greatly appreciated. Always loving and supportive. A special mention to my uncle Mark Mickan and aunty Pat Mickan (my mum's brother and sister). Growing up you taught me what hard work is. Seeing you play at the highest level of sport was what inspired me to pursue the same dream. Although I reached a reasonable level, I feel that work ethic has held me in good stead for wanting to make a serious difference in the world. And it certainly needed to be called on, in the writing of this book.

To Robert Hoff, you have had the greatest influence over my education career without a doubt. I am not sure what impresses me more, the fact you look the same in your twenties as you do at 70 or your dedication to education and, most importantly, your dedication to the wellbeing of our young people. Hoffy, you are a total legend. I remember that Sunday evening when I was at the Grand Hotel on a school night with a few mates when you and Sandra walked past. You excitedly doubled back to come in and say hello, but you were stopped by security, who said, 'Sorry mate, you're too old to come in'. Your response: 'My son is in there and he forgot his wallet'—and you calmly strolled past security. One of the more amusing things I have seen. Although this story has little to do with the book, it does demonstrate your support and willingness to go above and beyond.

In all seriousness, this book wouldn't exist if it wasn't for you Hoffy. When school returned in 2014, I went and saw you and explained the passion project I had started over the holidays. Instead of discouraging and questioning if it would take away from my teaching, you gave me the opposite response. You supported and encouraged me to get after it. And I remember sitting in your office at the end of 2016 like it was yesterday. I had taken a year's leave of absence from Immanuel to focus on Growing with Gratitude full time and I had to make the life-defining decision of whether to resign and make GWG my career. From a business sense, being a self-funded start-up, the funds weren't exactly flowing freely at the time. Sitting in your office, you asked, 'So what are you going to do?' My response was, 'I'm not sure'. The key moment was when you looked at me from across the table and said; 'You've come too far with this, give it your all and the worst thing that will happen is you go back and teach somewhere'. I'll be forever grateful for that bit of advice. Your knowledge and contribution to this book is also greatly appreciated. And the best thing: your mateship continues to this day.

Thank you so much to you, Nadia. You believed I could make GWG happen from day one. Your support in the early years is so greatly appreciated.

Thank you, thank you, thank you to you Lucy Raymond and Leigh McLennon (Wiley). I am so grateful to you both. Thank you for believing in me and the need to write a book on implementing gratitude in schools and family homes. Your patience, support, encouragement and feedback over the journey has been tremendous. A big thank you to all the Wiley team who helped bring this book to life including Chris Shorten, Renee Aurish, Ingrid Bond and everyone behind the scenes.

I am also extremely grateful to you, Dale Sidebottom. You were the first person to plant the seed in my mind about writing a book. You have been an amazing support through this whole process. I always love and look forward to the workshops we run together. I value your mateship highly, and your book *All Work No Play* (also published by Wiley) is brilliant.

I want to deeply express my appreciation to Shawn Kasbergen, Brenton Willson, Desy Pantelos, Mark Butler, Meagan Hart, Reid Dobson, Coreta Lennon, Anne-Marie Schmidt, Donna Safralidis, Michael Toogood, Colette Bos, Ben Storer, Ben Catalano, Dr Rachel Dodge, Luke Bartlett, Kurt Ferguson, Mark Steed Andrew Mittiga, Brett Humphrys, Kate Cameron, Dana Kerford, Ana Dominguez, Jamila MacArthur, Jessica Hertz, Alison Jamieson and Paula Luethen for sharing elements of your schools and your own wellbeing practices. It means so much that you took the time to respond by email, or to sit down with me in person or via Zoom to talk about the finer details. It's your personal stories that bring this book to life and help others see how they too can do similar practices.

I also want to express my gratitude to the brilliant minds of the academics I've worked with over the journey so far. Academia isn't my thing, yet I know how important it is to provide an evidence-based program. Thank you so much to Dr Debbie Price and Dr Deborah Green of the University of South Australia for your dedication to research in the mental wellbeing space in schools. And to Jasmine Turner, Psychology PhD candidate of The University of Adelaide. It's a privilege that you chose to do your three-year thesis on Growing with Gratitude.

I don't think Growing with Gratitude and I would have the presence we do today without some of the amazing partnerships we've formed over the years. I want to show my appreciation to the Adelaide Football Club (AFL team) and the community team who became our first ever major partnership. In 2014, the late great Jason Lehmann, Brooke Jeffs and Nigel Osborn and I sat around a table to discuss how Growing with Gratitude could potentially be the club's flagship community school engagement program. At the time, there was no GWG website and nothing was being delivered in schools. What was presented, though, was a dodgy PowerPoint and a real passion for wanting to teach skills of gratitude and other positive habits to young people. What better way to do that, than to partner with the biggest organisation in South Australia? Well, something went right because the Crows community team thought it was brilliant and exactly what they were looking for. To the late Jason 'Lehmo' Lehmann, Brooke Jeffs, Nigel Osborn, Brayden Kirk, Sam Tharaldsen and all the club's GWG presenters over the journey, I am just so grateful for your dedication and seriously good presenting skills. No doubt this book wouldn't have happened if it wasn't for your dedication to spreading the mental wellbeing message. Thank you.

I greatly appreciate you, Becckey Ernst: you are a tremendous research assistant. Thank you for your time and the effort you put in. And to Hayley, my gym buddy, who encouraged me to use 'big words' in the book: I think I managed two.

Sandra Balonyi: you are an amazing editor and I am so grateful to you. Your editing skills and advice are world class. It's amazing how the world works. We first met at a workshop in 2021, prior to me even considering writing this book. And now you're the editor. Your work is greatly appreciated.

To John Mannion and his dedicated team at BreakThrough Mental Health Research Foundation. Your support, insights and conversations are always inspiring. In such a short time the foundation is leading the way into funding mental health research. I look forward to many more of our conversations.

To all the schools and teachers from around the world who have embraced GWG and me: I am so grateful to you. At the time of writing, we've reached more than 800 schools in 45 countries to help young people grow with gratitude. That still astounds me! I can't wait for those numbers to grow even more.

I wrote most of the book in my favourite coffee shop, He Said She Said in Hyde Park. A huge thanks to Nizar, Sam, Maddy and the team for your incredible hospitality and tremendous long blacks with a dash of cold milk.

Rodney Love of rodneylovedesign.com.au: I am proud to call you a mate, and you're also the best graphic designer around, and he's responsible for bringing the Kilkenny Crew and the Grangers to life. During this book-writing process, I'd often call on Rodney for ideas, as his creative mind is brilliant. He's also responsible for all the branding for Growing with Gratitude and my personal brand website. Rodney, your mateship is greatly appreciated.

Friends are so important in our life and I feel lucky to have tremendous friends. They all were extremely supportive during the book writing process. A huge thanks to Jarrad Tait, Shaun Tait, Joe 'Pegleg' Hill, Luke Timmons, Shane Dunstall, Brendan Dunstall, Shane Berkett, Shane Kenney, Jordan Ausserlechner, Tom Hateley, Ben Warren, Nick Warren, Phil Cleggett, Scott Schubert, Russell 'General' Godson, Luke van Kempen and Carl Mickan

Last, and certainly not least, I am truly grateful to you, Kelly Irving. Working with you as my book coach has been an utter delight. When we started working together, you helped form a much clearer structure and flow to the book. Your knowledge and skills on writing are exceptional. There's no doubt this book wouldn't have been done without you. You are appreciated to the highest level.

As Australian boxing legend Jeff Fenech famously said, I love youse all.

Ash

CONNECT WITH ME

Thank you for taking action and the time to read this book and allowing me the opportunity to share my knowledge about implementing gratitude and the other positive habits into schools, classrooms and your home. It shows you care deeply about your own wellbeing, your loved ones and our next generation of young people.

Free Resource Pack

If you haven't already accessed the free Resource Pack mentioned throughout the book, be sure to head over to book.growingwithgratitude.com.au. There's a stack of games, activities, lessons, frameworks and display posters. They are perfect for your school and family home.

The Positive Education Podcast

The purpose of the podcast is for you to take away ideas that you can execute in your classroom, across your school, at your sports club and in your organisation, plus tips and tricks that you can apply in your own life. You'll hear stories, information and actionable ideas from positive education and wellbeing experts, school leaders, wellbeing co-ordinators and teachers. **ashmanuel.com/podcast**

Teacher and education training

If you'd love to work directly with me, there are a number of opportunities. At Growing with Gratitude, we deliver in-person teacher training at schools and we run events for educators to attend. We also run student workshops and in-class sessions both nationally and internationally.

Clubs and coaching

You also might be interested in our work with junior sports clubs, where we help clubs and coaches implement skills of gratitude and other positive habits into training sessions and matches. Also, check out our multi-sports program for 3–5-year-olds and young people with delayed development; and we also now work with tradies and corporates because at the end of the day it doesn't matter if you're a 3-year-old or 103-year-old, gratitude doesn't discriminate.

I wish you all the best on your gratitude journey! Come and connect and say hi!

Website: growingwithgratitude.com.au and ashmanuel.com

Email: info@growingwithgratitude.com.au

LinkedIn: ashmanuel

Instagram: @growingwithgratitude

Facebook: facebook.com/growingwithgratitude

If you loved this book and want to practise a gratitude act, then please leave a kind review online, or gift a copy to a friend, school or parent.

This is one small step towards growing a culture of wellbeing for us all.

Thank you!

SOURCES AND RESOURCES

This section includes a comprehensive list of references and citations from each chapter in the book.

Introduction

Australian National University 2021, 'COVID-19 taking bigger toll on kids' mental health', viewed 22 January 2022, https://bit .ly/3McKfBa

BreakThrough Mental Health Research Foundation 2022, 'We are facing the biggest health crisis of our lifetime', viewed 11 March 2022, https://breakthroughfoundation.org.au

McCarthy, N. 2020 'COVID-19's staggering impact on global education', viewed 4 December 2021, www.weforum.org/ agenda/2020/03/infographic-covid19-coronavirus-impact-global-education-health-schools

Chapter 1

Bott, D., Hoare, E. & Robinson J. 2017a, 'Learn it, live it, teach it, embed it: Implementing a whole school approach to foster positive mental health and wellbeing through Positive Education', viewed 12 January 2022, https:// internationaljournalofwellbeing.org/index.php/ijow/ article/view/645

Chowdbury, M. 2022, 'The neuroscience of gratitude and how it affects anxiety & grief', viewed 2 March 2022, https://positivepsychology.com/neuroscience-of-gratitude

Fell, A. 2018, 'Research reveals shocking new statistics of Australia's bullying', viewed 14 March 2022, https://mccrindle.com.au/insights/blog/three-in-five-australian-students-have-experienced-bullying

Lyubomirsky, S. 2008, *The how of happiness: A new approach to getting the life you want*, Penguin Press, New York.

NSW Government 2020a, 'Why student voice matters', viewed 17 February 2022, https://education.nsw.gov.au/student-wellbeing/student-voices/student-voice-and-leadership/why-student-voice-matters

Salavera, C., Usán, P., Teruel, P., Urbón, E. & Murillo, V. 2021 'School bullying: Empathy among perpetrators and victims', viewed 22 January 2022, https://doi.org/10.3390/su13031548

Seligman, M. 2013, 'Well-being & education: An introduction', viewed 26 April 2022, https://www.mtbhs.sa.edu.au/positive_education/resources

The University of Australia, 'Dr. Deborah Price', viewed 22 January 2022, https://people.unisa.edu.au/debbie.price

Chapter 2

Antliff, S. 2021, 'Workplace overwhelm: How to protect your team from change fatigue', viewed 6th July 2022, Atlassian. https://bit.ly/3ytnqWA

Dearing, J. 2009, 'Applying diffusion of innovation theory to intervention development', viewed 17 December 2021, www.ncbi.nlm.nih.gov/pmc/articles/PMC2957672

Dodge, R., Daly, A., Huyton, J. & Sanders, L. 2012, 'The challenge of defining wellbeing', viewed 25 January 2021,

International Journal of Wellbeing, www.international
journalofwellbeing.org/index.php/ijow/article/view/89/238

Gerard, M. 2009, 'Innovation and early adopters: Beyond
the bell curve', viewed 17 December 2021, https://apenotes
.wordpress.com/2009/08/29/innovation-and-early-adopters-
beyond-the-bell-curve

NSW Government 2020b, 'Why student voice matters', viewed
17 February 2022, https://education.nsw.gov.au/student-
wellbeing/student-voices/student-voice-and-leadership/
why-student-voice-matters

Runions, K.C., Pearce, N. & Cross, D. 2021a, 'How can schools
support whole-school wellbeing? A review of the research'.
Report prepared for the Association of Independent Schools of
New South Wales, viewed 20 April 2022, https://www.aisnsw
.edu.au/Resources/WAL%204%20%5BOpen%20Access%5D/
AISNSW%20Wellbeing%20Literature%20Review.pdf.

AINSW. 2022, 'Whole-school wellbeing', viewed 27 May
2022, https://www.aisnsw.edu.au/teachers-and-staff/
supporting-students/wellbeing

Singer, L. 2019, 'Diffusion of innovation theory', viewed 15
December 2021, https://sphweb.bumc.bu.edu/otlt/mph-modules/
sb/behavioralchangetheories/behavioralchangetheories4.html

Steed, M. 2022, 'A strategic approach to student wellbeing',

Council of British International Schools, viewed 7 February
2022, http://www.cobis.org.uk/our-network/blog/blog-demo-
page/~board/blogs/post/a-strategic-approach-to-student-
wellbeing

White, A. & McCallum, F. 2021a, *Wellbeing and resilience
education: COVID-19 and its impact on education*, 1st Edition,
eBook, Routledge, London.

Chapter 3

Brabeck, M., Fry, S. & Jeffrey, J. 2016, 'Practice for knowledge acquisition (not drill and kill): Deigning activities with the goal of transferring knowledge', viewed 25 February 2022, https://docplayer.net/50311224-Practice-for-knowledge-acquisition-not-drill-and-kill.html

Clear, J. 2018, *Atomic Habits: An easy & proven way to build good habits & break bad ones*, Cornerstone, London.

Reconciliation Australia, Acknowledgement of Country and Welcome to Country, viewed 15 March 2022, www.reconciliation.org.au/acknowledgement-of-country-and-welcome-to-country

Runions, K.C., Pearce, N. & Cross, D. 2021b, 'How can schools support whole-school wellbeing? A review of the research. Report prepared for the Association of Independent Schools of New South Wales', viewed 2 January 2021, https://www.aisnsw.edu.au/Resources/WAL%204%20%5BOpen%20Access%5D/AISNSW%20Wellbeing%20Literature%20Review.pdf

AINSW. 2022, 'Whole-school wellbeing', viewed 27 May 2022, https://www.aisnsw.edu.au/teachers-and-staff/supporting-students/wellbeing

Chapter 4

Ackermann, C. 2022a, '28 benefits of gratitude & most significant research findings', viewed 26 February 2022, https://positivepsychology.com/benefits-gratitude-research-questions

Ackermann, C. 2022b, 'What is gratitude and why is it so important?, viewed 27 February 2022, https://positivepsychology.com/gratitude-appreciation

Breuning, L. 2016, 'How to train your brain to go positive instead of negative', viewed 18 December 2021, www.forbes.com/sites/womensmedia/2016/12/21/how-to-train-your-brain-to-go-positive-instead-of-negative/?sh=51d0f7495a58

Career One 2021, 'The 5 benefits of having a growth mindset', viewed 2 December 2021, www.careerone.com.au/career-advice/career/the-5-benefits-of-having-a-growth-mindset-3036

Collins Dictionary, 'Definition of empathy', viewed 16 January 2022, www.collinsdictionary.com/dictionary/english/empathy

Green, D., Price, D., Manuel A. & Morrison A. 2015, 'Growing with gratitude' viewed 3 January 2022, https://www.acsa.edu.au/pages/images/D%20Green%20GWG.pdf

Holbrook, C. 'The power of kindness: Why being nice benefits us all', viewed 17 January 2022, www.happiness.com/magazine/science-psychology/benefits-of-kindness

Marquardt, D. 2020, 'Thriving in crisis: Serving others', viewed 8 March 2022, https://blogs.acu.edu/lytlecenter/2020/03/21/thriving-in-cr

Mayo Medical Staff 2022, 'Positive thinking: Stop negative self-talk to reduce stress', viewed 1 March 2022, www.mayoclinic.org/healthy-lifestyle/stress-management/in-depth/positive-thinking/art-20043950

Moore, C. 2022, 'What is negativity bias and how can it be overcome?', viewed 5 March 2022, https://positivepsychology.com/3-steps-negativity-bias

Oxford Learner's Dictionary, 'Definition of kindness', viewed 16 January 2022, www.oxfordlearnersdictionaries.com/definition/american_english/kindness

Rowland, M. 'Kindness matters guide', viewed 17 January 2022, www.mentalhealth.org.uk/campaigns/kindness/kindness-matters-guide

Salavera, C., Usán, P., Teruel, P., Urbón, E. & Murillo, V. 2021 'School bullying: Empathy among perpetrators and victims', viewed 22 January 2022, https://doi.org/10.3390/su13031548

The Decision Lab, 'Why is the news always so depressing? Negativity bias, explained', viewed 3 March 3 2022, https://thedecisionlab.com/biases/negativity-bias

Chapter 5

Achor, S. 2013, 'The happiness advantage key takeaways', viewed 5 December 2021, www.shawnachor.com/happiness-advantage-key-takeaways

Cassie of Teach Starter 2021, '5 Steps to using classroom reward systems in a meaningful way', viewed 18 February 2022, www.teachstarter.com/au/blog/classroom-reward-systems-and-intrinsic-motivation

Chazin, K. & Ledford, J. 2016, 'Class-wide reward systems': Evidence-based instructional practices for young children with autism and other disabilities. viewed 18 February 2022, http://ebip.vkcsites.org/class-wide-reward-systems

Emmons, R. 2010, 'Why gratitude is good', viewed 17 December 2021, https://greatergood.berkeley.edu/article/item/why_gratitude_is_good

Gilles Street Primary School, 'The intensive English language program', viewed 10 March 2022, www.gillesstps.sa.edu.au/IELP

Goldberg, J.M., Sklad, M. Elfrink, T.R. 2018, 'Effectiveness of interventions adopting a whole school approach to enhancing social and emotional development: A meta-analysis', viewed 5 March 2022, https://link.springer.com/article/10.1007/s10212-018-0406-9

Lean, C. & Leslie, M. 2020, 'Interoception, parent and caregiver booklet', Department for Education, South Australia, viewed 4 March 2022, www.education.sa.gov.au/sites/default/files/interoception-parent-caregiver-booklet.pdf

Nguyen, H. 2021, 'How to use gameplay to enhance classroom learning', viewed 19 December 2021, www.edutopia.org/article/how-use-gameplay-enhance-classroom-learning

NSW Government 2021a, 'Explicit teaching practices and feedback', viewed 26 February 2022, https://education.nsw.gov.au/student-wellbeing/tell-them-from-me/accessing-and-using-tell-them-from-me-data/tell-them-from-me-measures/explicit-teaching-practices-and-feedback

Sidebottom, D. 2021, *All Work No Play: A surprising guide to feeling more mindful, grateful & cheerful*, 1st edition, Wiley, Melbourne.

Terada, Y. 2018, 'Dos and don'ts of classroom decorations: What you put on your classroom walls can affect your students' ability to learn', viewed 21 December 2021, www.edutopia.org/article/dos-and-donts-classroom-decorations

Chapter 6

Broom, C. 2015, 'Empowering students: Pedagogy that benefits educators and learners', viewed 26 February 2022, https://journals.sagepub.com/doi/pdf/10.1177/2047173415597142#

Centre for Education Statistics & Evaluation, NSW Government 2020, 'Supporting students' sense of belonging synthesis paper', viewed 21 January 2022, https://education.nsw.gov.au/about-us/educational-data/cese/publications/research-reports/supporting-students-sense-of-belonging

NSW Government 2020c, 'Why student voice matters', viewed 17 February 2022, https://education.nsw.gov.au/student-wellbeing/student-voices/student-voice-and-leadership/why-student-voice-matters

Soul Pancake, 'An experiment in gratitude: The science of happiness', https://youtu.be/oHv6vTKD6lg

Washington State University 2019, 'Weekly tip: Ownership of learning', viewed 21 January 2022, https://li.wsu.edu/2019/01/25/ownership-of-learning

Chapter 7

Binder, M. & Freytag, A. 2013, 'Volunteering, subjective well-being and public policy', viewed 17 December 2022, www.mtbhs.sa.edu.au/positive_education/resources

Boothby, S. 2017, 'Does music affect your mood?', viewed 9 December 2022, www.healthline.com/health-news/mental-listening-to-music-lifts-or-reinforces-mood-051713

Burke, R. & Swaine, M. 2022, 'Wellbeing around the world: Giving staff extra time off', viewed 9 March 2022, www.tes.com/magazine/leadership/staff-management/wellbeing-around-world-giving-staff-extra-time

Bushby, M. 2019, 'Teachers experience more stress than other workers, study shows, viewed 4 March 2022, www.theguardian.com/education/2019/feb/25/teachers-experience-more-stress-than-other-workers-study-shows

Cross, D, 'Teacher wellbeing and its impact on student learning', viewed 19 January 2022, https://www.research.uwa.edu.au/__data/assets/pdf_file/0010/2633590/teacher-wellbeing-and-student.pdf

Health Direct 2020, 'Exercise and mental health', viewed 9 December 2022, www.healthdirect.gov.au/exercise-and-mental-health

Go Volunteer, https://govolunteer.com.au

Henebery, B. 2021, 'A profession in distress: 84 per cent of teachers think of quitting', viewed 3 March 2022, www.theeducatoronline.com/k12/news/a-profession-in-distress-84-of-teachers-think-of-quitting/279048

Locczak, H. 2022, 'Humor in psychology: Coping and laughing your woes away', viewed 22 February 2022, https://positivepsychology.com/humor-psychology

Sinek, S. 2017, *Leaders Eat Last: Why some teams pull together and others don't*, Portfolio Penguin, London.

Stroud, G. 2017, 'Why do teachers leave?', viewed 3 March 2022, www.abc.net.au/news/2017-02-04/why-do-teachers-leave/ 8234054

Sutton, A. 2016, 'Measuring the effects of self-awareness: Construction of the self-awareness outcomes questionnaire', viewed 27 February, www.ncbi.nlm.nih.gov/pmc/articles/ PMC5114878

Szabo, A. 2003, 'The acute effects of humor and exercise on mood and anxiety', viewed 22 February 2022, www.nrpa .org/globalassets/journals/jlr/2003/volume-35/jlr-volume-35- number-2-pp-152-162.pdf

Willink, J. & Babin, L. 2015, *Extreme ownership: How U.S. navy seals lead and win*, St Martin's Press, Chicago.

The future is now

Bott, D., Hoare, E. & Robinson J. 2017b, 'Learn it, live it, teach it, embed it: Implementing a whole school approach to foster positive mental health and wellbeing through Positive Education', viewed 12 January 2022, https://international journalofwellbeing.org/index.php/ijow/article/view/645/625

Brainy Quote, Henry Adams, viewed 11 March 2022, www .brainyquote.com/quotes/henry_adams_108018

Hare, J. 2022, 'Be happy! School success will follow', viewed 9 March 2022, www.afr.com/work-and-careers/education/ be-happy-school-success-will-follow-20220208-p59usk

NSW Government 2021b, 'Explicit teaching practices and feedback', viewed 11 March 2022, https://education.nsw.gov .au/student-wellbeing/tell-them-from-me/accessing-and- using-tell-them-from-me-data/tell-them-from-me-measures/ explicit-teaching-practices-and-feedback

White, A. & McCallum, F. 2021b, 'Wellbeing and resilience education: COVID-19 and its impact on education' 1st Edition, eBook, Routledge, London.

HELPFUL RESOURCES

LifeLine

13 11 14

lifeline.org.au

Beyond Now

beyondblue.org.au/get-support/beyondnow-suicide-safety-planning

Head to Health

headtohealth.gov.au

SANE Australia

1800 187 263

sane.org/services/help-centre

Lifeline Service Finder

lifeline.serviceseeker.com.au

Black Dog Institute

blackdoginstitute.org.au

BreakThrough Mental Health Research Foundation

breakthroughfoundation.org.au

For students

BRAVE

brave-online.com

Kids Helpline

1800 55 1800

kidshelpline.com.au

MoodGYM:

moodgym.com.au

Youthbeyondblue

youthbeyondblue.com

INDEX